ADVANCE PRAISE FOR *Footprint*

"This amazing and original book is something of a global/time travel walking tour with anti-colonialism, land rights, and activist art among its many subtexts. Each 'itinerary' follows trails and maps into another unbeaten track, another unfamiliar corner of our world. From impressions on the earth to human anatomy to empathetic microhistories ranging from Cinderella and Winnie the Pooh to the shoe industry, urban sidewalks, war, and ICE (to mention only a few), Radhika Subramaniam's impressive scholarship and lovely writing asks in so many ways 'What's the next step?'" —Lucy R. Lippard

"A transdisciplinary gazetteer traversing histories of labor and cultural memory, violence and physical persistence, *Footprint* invites us to track this seemingly simple trace all over the world, time out of mind—from the ground at Laetoli, 3.66 million years ago, near the Olduvai Gorge in what is now Tanzania, to the edge of the Sea of Tranquility on the moon, in 1969, and on to the landscape of carbon expenditure in the Anthropocene. We have been here—and there, and there—and, like Crusoe, met ourselves coming and going, as a feared and longed-for other. The human footprint, writes Subramaniam, is 'not an inert carrier; it is an elemental encounter.' Her book stages that encounter, delicately and indelibly." —Frances Richard, Senior Editor, *Places Journal*

"*Footprint* puts the politics back into walking, linking it to a poetics of marking. In a wonderful array of examples drawn from colonial Mexico to post-riot Brixton, from Hopi philosophy to the decipherment (and reburial) of ancient tracks from the Willandra Lakes, Subramaniam shows how footing, as mobile cartography, as resistance to tarmac, as path-making, as the refusal of all kinds of standardisation, rethinks the foundations

of co-existence. Just as no foot walks alone, we track ourselves (as others track us): in her dazzlingly diverse and pedagogically irresistible stories, footprints are the measure of migration. Owning movement, they put the choreography back into geography. And the ethics. A brilliant essay in eco-poetics, engagingly therapeutic for a culture whose sedentarism has left feet dragging behind."
—Paul Carter, author of *The Road to Botany Bay* and Professor of Design (Urbanism), RMIT University, Melbourne

"*Footprint: Four Itineraries* is a guidepost to a world alive with the tactile matterings of elemental encounters. An opening into the endless tales of footprints that surface on sidewalks, deserts, and the moon. Footprints here are worldly stories on a constellation of paths. Leaden, light, persistent, dreamy, and differently infused, they are waylaid by war, or they manifest, in their way, the cruel greed of imperialism or the curiosity of a world walked. Ordinary, ubiquitous, and oddly self-evident, footprints are at once palpable and buoyant, carrying the pleasures and fears of what was left behind and what propelled people or elephants into the promise of different horizons. Ephemeral, they cede ground to what comes after.

Subramaniam's beautiful and brilliant work is itself an enigmatic imprint made of words and images that call out impacts, dwell in a temporality, follow a footprint's humble claim. The book is not about footprints but travels with them across histories, technologies, and affects.

Asking if it is yet possible to tread lightly on our world, Subramaniam moves alongside artists and cartographers and feet into the glitchy heart of the real, performing the weight of a world riven with the horror and generativity of ambition and still standing."
—Kathleen Stewart, author of Ordinary Affects and Professor Emerita, University of Texas, Austin.

"*Footprint: Four Itineraries* is a fascinating untangling of the metaphors and meanings accrued around the marks made by feet. From colonial mapping to border guard tracking, the first steps on the moon to inclusive prosthetics, the Kartini Kendeng cement protests in Indonesia to Mona Hatoum's performance art, the book moves through time, around the world, and into space, arguing for the liveliness and the mobility of the footprint (and the vitality of human-scale motion)."
—Clare Qualmann, Associate Professor, University of East London and Co-Founder, Walking Artists Network

"Intellectually omnivorous and playful, *Footprint* invites the reader to explore the footprint as material artifact and as a site for the production of meanings: from Robinson Crusoe's shock encountering a single footprint on his island, to the dusty impressions left by the first astronauts on the moon, to Aboriginal trackers who were employed to hunt down fugitive white convicts in early nineteenth-century Australia."
—Charles Zerner, Cohn Professor of Environmental Studies Emeritus, Sarah Lawrence College

FOOTPRINT

Essays
in the
Critical
Humanities

Series Editorial Collective
Hosam Aboul-Ela / Cynthia Franklin / Greta LaFleur /
Louis Mendoza / S. Shankar / Neferti X. M. Tadiar

Footprint

Four Itineraries

Radhika Subramaniam

np:

np:
np-press.org

© 2025 by Radhika Subramaniam

All rights reserved.

ISBN 978-1-962365-05-5

Library of Congress Cataloging in Publication Data is available.

Cover image by the author

For Nissim,
footprints-in-the-making

CONTENTS

GUIDEPOST   1

Itinerary 1: Stride   5

*Lift-off—Route/Boot—Metaphor/Material—
Making/Taking*

Itinerary 2: Pace   31

*In Step and Out of Step—Atlas and Abstraction—
Fitting Cinderella*

Itinerary 3: Trudge   58

*Pounding the Pavement—Edifice/Embodiment—
Boots on the Ground/Shoes in the Air—Cement Shoes—
Brick Feet—War Un-memorial*

Itinerary 4: Track   88

*Unsettling—Foundation—Crusoe's Dreaming—
Tracking—Migration and Memory—Eluding Capture*

GUIDEPOST   113

Acknowledgments   115

Bibliography   117

GUIDEPOST

Consider the following footprints: those drawn by indigenous artists in maps of New Spain created for the Spanish crown; the footprint impressed on the moon as "one small step for man" in 1969; and today's carbon "footprint." The prints on the Spanish maps make visible within imperial cartography the lifeways that were being violently obliterated under colonial rule. The thrilling moonwalks of Apollo 11 came with the freight of Cold War geopolitics, U.S. imperial ambitions, and the disregard of racial, social, and economic inequities at home. And for all that the carbon footprint intends to hold to account the totality of anthropogenic action, it encodes and obscures the asymmetries between the global North and South with their historically different carbon emissions. Each footprint spotlights an instance of human politics and questions of social justice embedded in the histories and practices of colonialism, U.S. imperialism, capitalism, and racial, economic, and environmental disparities.

While that clarity is bracing, it is illusory. The footprint so constructed is an object, a fixed event or moment in time, but this assumed legibility comes at the cost of masking the footprint's mobility—not only is it formed in motion, it carries with it other trajectories, ideas, people, and histories. Every footstep tempts those who follow to pour interpretation into its print and to cement meaning. This predilection to see the footprint as the stable imprint of a foot's tread, an artifact that claims space, rather than as a brush with movement, has significant implications. Customary usages in eco-politics as much as in architecture produce the footprint as a static and substantial form. Footprints struggle to leave a visible trace on city streets where their authority has been seized by buildings. Feet are evacuated from terrain they once trekked and surveyed into the distanced lines and coordinates of maps. Although derived from bodies, feet begin to discipline us as external standards of measurement.

The footprint's corporeal basis makes it both familiar and easy for anyone to visualize and therefore, not unexpectedly, it pops up everywhere—thoroughly mundane, a sentimental cliché, a lazy metaphor. But its ubiquity also means that it remains unexamined whether evoked in the metaphors of carbon and building footprints, or whether as a physical trace too frequently absorbed into pre-existing evidentiary and museological paradigms. The result is that we no longer see the footprint as such, let alone sense that it was born in a process of imprinting.

This book unsettles the fixity of the footprint to take it for a walk. In doing so, it demonstrates that while the footprint is a recurrent and persistent image that signifies presence whether of human or divine, of otherness, or of prey, the ways in which its meanings are woven into being and how they unravel and migrate vary. Exploring the multivalent and ambiguous ways in which the footprint has surfaced, it probes what we can learn from the ways in which it has been deployed, perhaps fostering another relationship with the world.

Are there other lineages of the footprint, humbler and formed in relation, to follow in whose footsteps would promise different horizons?

The footprints within this book take many forms—sly, bold, heavy, faint, light, obscured, humble, confused, uncertain, persistent—and they appear across a rich landscape from maps to monuments to mythology to the moon. The book offers four itineraries, each of which twines the heterogeneous and enigmatic ways in which the foot moves and the footprint surfaces. Feet and their prints are no more separated from one another than our bodies and their imaginations, and just as the ground onto which feet step remains inextricable from the prints that form on it. Even as the journeys range from colonial cartography to the standardization of measurement, from religious iconography to artistic practice, from literature to the policing of borders, from the politics of memory to prosthetics, the itineraries are not *about* the footprints found therein; rather, they travel *with* footprints to bring into view the intersections, collisions, and contradictions of this very material metaphor.

You can start at the first itinerary and follow the journeys to the end but you can also dip in and out, winding image and idea together to create your own paths and series of footprints. The itineraries are inevitably partial; they meander, loop, and follow each other's trails, resisting a too-quick assessment of where we are going. In that sense, this is a travel book that invites you to travel with, wander off, or to invite other footprints in to share the path of inquiry. After all, many traditions have understood the footprint as something held in common rather than an intrepid individual claim to the open road or a solo discovery. Shared footprints sketch paths that resist being inked in, insisting that we continually draft them along with, and in the steps of, others in a continual process of drawing and re-drawing them together.

ITINERARY 1

STRIDE

Lift-off

The first human footprints on the moon, made just over fifty years ago, are likely to last for millions of years. The moon has none of the tempestuous volcanism, tides, and waves that characterize our own blue sphere. In its airless, waterless environment, there is little to disturb those imprints. *What were your inner feelings?* asked the eager press of the astronauts of Apollo 11, uncertain how to phrase their question. *Did you feel you were stepping on a piece of the earth, on something like a desert perhaps or was it clearly another world?*[1] How easy it is to understand their curiosity and confusion. After all, what is a small step, let alone a giant leap, when it's not on the ground beneath our feet?

The first photographs of the lunar surface appeared in *The New York Times* ten days after the moon landing of 1969 under the headline "Footprints on the Moon."[2] They show the U.S. flag and a mess of footprints around it. Although there was some discussion as to whether planting a flag might be construed as an

---

1. *New York Times*, "Questions and Answers."
2. *New York Times*, "Footprints."

overreaching territorial claim, a burgeoning national pride overcame such objections. Space flight and NASA's related technological ambitions were fueled by the Space Race of the Cold War. The Soviet Union's competitive advantage mounted in 1961 when cosmonaut Yuri Gagarin became the first human to orbit the earth. President John F. Kennedy's declaration before Congress that year to land "a man on the moon" and return him safely to Earth galvanized the efforts of the U.S.'s relatively young space agency. In his 1962 address to Rice University in Houston (more often remembered as the "we choose to go to the moon" speech) Kennedy avowed, "we shall not see it governed by a hostile flag of conquest, but by a banner of freedom and peace. We have vowed that we shall not see space filled with weapons of mass destruction, but with instruments of knowledge and understanding."[3] The only way these vows could be fulfilled, he went on to add, was if the U.S. was first to get there. Primacy was undoubtedly the flag's claim.

Congress passed a bill after the fact indicating that the planting of the flag was only a symbolic gesture of national achievement, not one of appropriation. Getting the symbolism into a photogenic position required some doing. No flag could flutter on the airless moon—to ensure that the star-spangled banner yet waved, it had to be wired.[4] The enduring symbolism of the accompanying footprints, however, has required neither manipulation nor congressional reassurance. To be accurate, they are bootprints. In close-up, they appeared perfectly cast, delineating the horizontal treads of the astronauts' overshoes. Edwin "Buzz" Aldrin, one of the two moonwalkers, acknowledged that their feet sank

3. Kennedy, "John F. Kennedy Moon Speech."
4. NASA, "Flag Day."

Stride / 7

Bootprint on the lunar surface, Apollo 11 mission, July 20, 1969. Courtesy: NASA.

in a little on the moon's surface. Where the surface was flat, the foot penetrated a scant quarter or half an inch but near the crater rims or on the slopes, it could be several inches.[5] The resulting strong impression, strangely at home, signified a contact whose bold magnitude was thrilling.

To describe how the prints were made, an astrogeologist associated with NASA, the appositely named Gene Shoemaker,

---

5. *New York Times*, "Questions and Answers."

used a familiar earthly image: much like sand on a beach, he said, the lunar surface had some strength.[6] On this tensile layer, feet wouldn't sink in and prints disappear as they might in a liquid. Rather, they would leave the sort of marks that have imprinted themselves as indelibly on our imaginations as on the sands of time—appearing on the surface of Tranquility Base as if on a tranquil terrestrial seashore. The moon itself would spin us back in time to the first cosmic ricochets that created the solar system, its arid airless world providing geological evidence from planetary infancy. Earth too bears the scars of this time, but the natural forces of eruption and erosion have significantly transformed its surface.

We are now well acquainted with the image of our blue and white, watery, cloudy planet seen from outer space. Among the most memorable photographs from the Apollo 11 mission was one of Earth with wisps of clouds over its continents and seas, looking uncannily as familiar as a globe spun on a schoolroom desktop. Years later, recalling the view from the moon, Neil Armstrong remembered seeing both Greenland as an expanse of icy white and the unmistakable contours of Africa, the sun glinting off a lake.[7] Right in that line of sight, just under a decade later, the footprints of our own early sojourn on this planet were unearthed. Paleoanthropologist Mary Leakey and her team excavated a set of footprints of our hominin ancestors at Laetoli, near the Olduvai Gorge of Tanzania.

The footprints, wrote Leakey, had the "rounded heel, uplifted arch, and forward pointing big toe of the human foot," unfalter-

---

6. *New York Times*, "Footprints."
7. Armstrong, "Oral History."

Footprints at Laetoli, Tanzania. Credit: John Reader/Science Photo Library.

ing evidence of early bipedalism.[8] Found amid many tracks of animals and birds, the three sets of prints, dating to about 3.6 million years ago, ran about 73 feet in a straight line. They seemed to suggest a group walking close together—two walking in tandem with the footsteps of the second placed within that of the leader, and another smaller set of prints alongside. All of them would have been smaller in stature than the modern human, ranging between 4 feet 1 inch to 4 feet 7 inches. As they walked, the smallest set seemed to stop and turn briefly before moving on, which Leakey remarked "gives the whole thing a very human aspect."[9] We can only speculate about what happened at this juncture, in this pivot of hesitation that feels as familiar to our feet as the directness of the forward pointed big toe. Was it a sudden onrush of caution or uncertainty? Or a wistful retrospect at the traces left behind before the group walked forward through the annals of evolution into the genus homo and out of Africa? Or was it simply an instant arrested by the sight of the silvery moon on which one day, another set of deep and determined prints would mirror those being left below?

About three decades after the Leakey excavation, in the late 2000s, another set of footprints was discovered in Ileret, Kenya.[10] Dating later, to about 1.5 million years ago, these are, as yet, the earliest prints found of genus homo, a foot that most closely resembles the modern human appendage. However, fossil evidence from East Asia, attributable to homo erectus, and dating even earlier, to 1.8 million years ago, demonstrates that our human

8. Hay and Leakey, "The Fossil Footprints of Laetoli," 56.
9. Rensberger, "Prehistoric Footprints."
10. Bennett et al., "Early Hominin Foot Morphology."

ancestors had long since migrated across the globe.[11] Bipedalism was once believed to have released our crafty hands and given us a bigger brain to go with it, but it appears to have preceded both. Mary Leakey acknowledged that no tools have been found in the vicinity of the Laetoli prints even though the walkers clearly had their hands free. The proximity of the footprints to each other suggests, in fact, that they were very probably using their arms and hands to hold each other.[12]

The creation and preservation of the human footprints at Laetoli alongside those of other animals such as hares, giraffes, elephants, and birds happened in a Goldilocks moment of a few weeks, between the dry season and the onset of rains. As with the moonprints, whose making Shoemaker described, the surface had to be simultaneously soft and cohesive. If the sand was too loose, it could register the light step of a bird's foot but a heavier one such as that of an elephant would soon start to collapse on the sides. If the substrate was too wet, it would retain the imprints of bigger, heavier animals but a lighter step would not sink in, nor would it register the rainprints that are also embedded in the Laetoli tuff. What captured the prints for millions of years was the result of the earth's volatility, impressed as they were into a thin layer of ash from a volcanic eruption most likely about fifteen miles away. Volcanic ash has the texture of fine or medium grained sand. Rain fell on the ash, creating the ideal substrate for the prints to form deeper impressions, and this mix had then congealed almost like plaster. Before they could be washed away or otherwise eroded, they had been buried by succeeding layers of ash, which preserved and protected them without adhering too closely, so that even-

11. Wilford, "Prints Show a Modern Foot in Prehumans."
12. Leakey, "Tracks and Tools."

tually the material would separate enough from the footprints to render them visible.[13]

Volcanic terrain is, in fact, the ideal counterpart to the lunar surface. Before the Apollo mission, the rocky volcanic landscape of Northern Arizona was selected to serve as the astronauts' practice grounds. The area was no stranger to extraterrestrial contact. It hadn't been that long since Gene Shoemaker had demonstrated that a large bowl-shaped crater near Flagstaff was the result of a collision with a meteor. Not far from Meteor Crater, NASA engineers blasted the ground at Cinder Lake to create a pock marked moonscape with cinder cones and hundreds of craters of different depths. Lunar orbiters were sent up periodically before the mission to photographically survey the surface of the moon, especially the potential landing sites. Using this imagery and their knowledge of cratering mechanics, the scientists of the U.S. Geological Survey were set to reproduce this terrain. First, they raked the surface, so it was smooth. Then, they set off explosive charges to create a 10-acre landscape analogous to the lunar one the astronauts would encounter, which would give them a sense of having "been there before."[14] Beyond providing familiarity, it also served to educate the astronauts, who were primarily pilots and engineers and not scientists, to enable them to approach the lunar environment knowledgeably. It was Shoemaker who was largely responsible for ensuring that there was both a scientific program in this man-on-the-moon venture and that it had the televisual component that was to leave a lasting impression on the minds of viewers across the world.[15] He was among the astrogeologists

---

13. Hay and Leakey, "The Fossil Footprints."
14. WGBH, "NOVA, to the Moon."
15. CBS News, "NASA May Not Have Televised."

who worked with the astronauts, teaching them how to identify geologic formations in this crater field and prepare for the other lunar features they might encounter when they took their first unearthly steps.

Buzz Aldrin missed the cues from his feet on the moonwalk. Weighing a sixth of his earthly weight with his foot landing neither long enough nor often enough on the surface, he found it hard to control his movements, slow down, or change course. Movement and direction had to be anticipated ahead of time.[16] Footprints are made in a critical conjuncture of pressure and impact, movement and propulsion against the composition and properties of the substrate. In the striding human foot, the heel hits the ground first, usually leaving the first deep impression. As the body shifts its weight forward, the lateral sides of the feet make their mark until momentum is surrendered to the balls of the feet, the metatarsal heads. The toes then exert their pressure, and the final "lift-off" is achieved as the big toe pushes against the ground. If the surface is soft, yet still tensile, and the atmosphere relatively calm, the walker leaves a trace. Many stories are contained in those traces—born of casual confidence, force, curiosity, desire, hesitancy, strain. The human stride, whose account is so often subservient to the hand, has made its own mark on our history. The fruits of our handiwork quite justly enjoy the focus of considerable attention. On the other hand, the products of our footfall are much harder to grasp, most discernible perhaps in the vast range of our migrations. But while the trace of our hands—the fingerprint—has been appropriated by the disciplinary apparatuses of the state, the footprint has been resolutely ambiguous,

---

16. *New York Times*, "Questions and Answers."; Also, WGBH, op. cit.

interpreted equally in terms of its impact as its sense of initiative. Simultaneously enigmatic and evocative, signifying both presence and absence, forceful yet transient, the footprint reveals an itinerant evidentiary history.

Route/Boot

There are other footprints on the land that was made unearthly to familiarize the astronauts. At the time of the first European *entrada* or incursion, it was territory inhabited mainly by Pueblo peoples. For Hopi, this was a land that had come into being through the material legacies of ancestral migration and settlement. As they tell it, when their ancestors emerged from the underworld into the Fourth Way of Life of our time, the lord of the Fourth World, Maasaw, greeted them. He taught them how to live on the land, how to form clans, and how to live alongside other beings. Instructing them to search for the center of their world, he enjoined them to make footprints as they travelled. From the umbilicus of their emergence, which some say is in the Grand Canyon, and others suggest is much farther south, the ancestors walked to the world's farthest corners, looping around until they made their home on the mesas of Northern Arizona. They learned the land with their feet, and as they did, they heeded Maasaw's injunction, *ang kuktota*, along there, make footprints.[17]

It wasn't just their feet that left traces, these footprints included the places they brought into being as they travelled onward to their present homes. All across the Fourth World are the signs of their migration—ruins, potsherds, petroglyphs, shrines, trails and

17. Colwell-Chanthaponh and Ferguson, "Memory Pieces and Footprints."; Kuwanwisiwma and Ferguson, "Ang Kuktota."; Kuwanwisiwma, Ferguson, and Colwell-Chanthaponh, eds., *Footprints of Hopi History*.

trail markers, sacred springs and other sites that mark their journey and the places in which they dwelled on the way. One such dwelling is in a cliffside in Southern Utah, where the Bears Ears buttes rise above Cedar Mesa, well to the north of the Hopi mesas of Arizona. Here, the old Puebloans once watched the moon eclipse the sun and plunge the earth into shadow.[18] Here, they transcribed that celestial sight onto an earthen wall in the crescent and circular pictographs that give the site its name, Moon House, and thereby imprinted onto its surface their own lunar experience.

To Hopi, these are *kukveni*—footprints—that assure the descendants of their makers that the land has been traversed as instructed. Hopi elders and scholars say that the covenant with Maasaw to make footprints obliges them to be stewards of these lands.[19] The potsherds, petroglyphs, and trail markers are not archaeological artifacts of a bygone world or even memorials to a past but footprints in a world that is alive in the here and now. These are lands that entered human time through a history of movement rather than settlement. The songs, stories, and rituals of the Hopi encode this history, not only connecting places and events across time but also across distances.[20]

Such footprints are not just symbols of a commemorative imagination, they are meant to be re-inscribed and re-invoked through the actual tracing of steps and trails. The actions undertaken by descendants of the ancient Puebloans preserve, we might say, not only the footfalls of the past or the steps being taken in the present but also the footprints to come. Hopi has a term

---

18. Boslough, "Is the Moon House an American Stonehenge."
19. Kuwanwisiwma and Ferguson, op. cit.
20. Colwell-Chanthaponh and Ferguson, op. cit.

for the act of looking for footprints: *kukhepya*. Hopi archaeologists and the archaeologists of the southwest who collaborate with them say that it is through kukhepya or looking for footprints that Hopi people recognize, understand and value their territory.[21] Of course, this territory extends beyond the limits of the reservation into which they were corralled; the footprints include places along their ancestral migration routes that stretch beyond Arizona to other parts of the U.S. (such as the Moon House on Cedar Mesa) and even into Mexico.

The areas through which the clans migrated were colonized and settled as part of the Spanish empire's ambitions in the so-called New World. In the sixteenth century, they formed part of the larger ambit of New Spain, a vast domain covering parts of both North and South America that was under the Spanish imperium. After the Mexican War of Independence, which liberated Mexico from Spain in 1821, they became part of Mexico until the U.S. annexation of Texas prompted a new round of hostilities a few decades later. The treaty of Guadalupe Hidalgo in 1848, which ended the Mexican-American war, led to a new apportioning of lands. With that treaty and the Gadsden Purchase thereafter, the U.S. gained all or part of today's Arizona, California, Colorado, New Mexico, Utah, and Wyoming and expanded its territories by over half a million square miles. Within a few decades, the Hopi reservation had been created in north-eastern Arizona by presidential executive order. It has shrunk even from its first arbitrary boundaries and today, the footprint it occupies is roughly 1.5 million acres or about 2,532 square miles. Other indigenous communities located farther south found that the new borderline

---

21. Ferguson, Berlin, and Kuwanwisiwma, "Kukhepya."

between the United States and Mexico established by the treaty cleaved their territories.

Today, the U.S. border itself has a sizeable footprint, extending beyond the established boundary line. Up to a hundred miles beyond the border, well north of designated ports of entry, U.S. Customs and Border Protection operate a system of checkpoints and patrols to create a border zone of surveillance. Within this zone, agents have extended search and seizure powers with the authority to stop, question, and detain people they suspect of being undocumented migrants or of committing other immigration violations. Along the almost 2,000-mile border between the two countries, a series of discrete barriers has been erected as "tactical infrastructure" to thwart ease of movement across the border. Colloquially called the "border wall" and even "border fence," these barriers are rarely at the actual borderline itself but placed farther back in U.S. territory. Near these border walls, Border Patrol agents continually scour the terrain for the tracks of border crossers, often dragging tires behind patrol vehicles to create a smooth surface on which fresh prints can be swiftly discerned. To evade detection, migrants themselves will sometimes wrap their shoes with fabric to avoiding leaving footprints.[22]

Kukhepya takes on new urgency when the re-inscription of footprints through regular journeys and ritual pilgrimages is disrupted. The incorporation of Pueblo lands into Spanish and Mexican colonial territory and then into the U.S. state has disturbed their physical traces, even when they continue to live in narrative and ritual. Trails have been obscured, eroded, merged into the roadway system, or otherwise taken over by the state or by private

---

22. Personal interview with Border Patrol Agent, Brownsville Texas, 2015.

A Border Patrol vehicle drags tires to smooth the ground so that footprints and other marks can be easily discerned. Brownsville, Texas. Photograph: Author, February 2015.

owners. Archaeologists report that some elders feel that identifying and documenting trails so that they can be managed through U.S. heritage or historic preservation compliance procedures is essential since they can no longer be looked after through routine use.[23] Footprints that are legacies of movement geographies, whether trails, natural features, markers, or former villages must therefore be solidified as national monuments, if they are not to risk complete erasure.

In 2016, after consultation with the tribes who regard it as an ancestral footprint, a presidential proclamation was issued by the

---

23. Ferguson, Berlin, and Kuwanwisiwma, op. cit.

Obama Administration designating Bears Ears a national monument. The very next year, another presidential proclamation from the next administration, that of Donald J. Trump, reduced its size to two small discrete parcels, diminishing protected land by 85%. In so doing, more of Bears Ears land was laid open to uranium mining and other extractive interests. Environmentalists, archaeologists, paleontologists, and indigenous groups rose in protest. In December 2017, an inter-tribal coalition of the Hopi, Zuni, Navajo, Ute, and Ute Mountain Ute Tribes filed a complaint against the Trump Administration to block further action. Among those who were quoted in the complaint was the vice-chairman of the Hopi tribe, Alfred Lomahquahu, who said, "Cedar Mesa is a part of our footprints, a path that tells a story. ... Those who have lived before us have never left."[24] Under the Biden Administration in 2021, a new review restored the territory.

Where the footprints of the country's first human inhabitants are under threat, the foot of the last conquistador has not been secure either. In 2017, as the Bears Ears Monument was radically slashed, another fractured monument emerged from the shadows. This was a bronze foot, intended to be solid and everlasting, severed from a statue of Don Juan de Oñate—the Spanish conquistador who established some of the earliest European settlements in what was to become New Mexico. In 1598, Don Juan led a group of soldiers and colonists north from Mexico to look for silver, gold, and other treasures. The terrain and climate were unfriendly, and the quest for precious metals futile, but Oñate pressed on with scant disregard for his followers or for the others they met on the way. The Spanish entered new territories under the *encomienda*

---

24. *Hopi Tribe et al vs. Donald J. Trump et al*, 23.

system, wherein they exacted labor and tribute from those who lived there to support and finance their conquests. Toward the Pueblo peoples who refused or resisted these preposterous demands, Oñate responded with such brutality that he was later hauled up before the Spanish Crown and convicted. His worst excesses were at Acoma Pueblo in New Mexico where he and his men slaughtered about eight hundred people and captured hundreds of men, women, and children. About two dozen men over the age of twenty-five were subjected to additional punishment—each one had his right foot cut off.

Competing conceptions of historical memory have shaped the figure of Oñate.[25] In the intervening centuries since his invasion, the narrative of the founding of the United States has narrowed to the English settlements of the eastern seaboard, so that the Spanish histories of the country, which date to a century before, have been obscured. Even as polyglot cultural worlds remain strong in the south and southwest, they have also been constructed as part of a borderland in which some long-term residents find themselves marginalized and rendered as foreign. In a struggle to define a place in the conception of nation, in a demonstration of Spanish heritage, and against the backdrop of an increasingly Anglicized narrative emanating from other parts of the country, efforts began to coalesce around the *cuarto centenario* or four hundredth anniversary of Oñate's *entrada*. In anticipation, in the mid-1990s, a statue of Don Juan was erected at Alcalde in the Española Valley of New Mexico, where the conquistador had established the earliest settlements.

Just before the anniversary year dawned, in the dark of night

---

25. See Brooke, "Conquistador Statue Stirs Hispanic Pride and Indian Rage," and Seefeldt, "Oñate's Foot."

on December 29, 1997, the statue's right foot was cut off. A letter arrived at the offices of the *Albuquerque Journal North* saying that the action had been done on behalf of the "brothers and sisters of Acoma Pueblo" and "in commemoration of the 400th anniversary of his unasked for exploration of our land."[26] No one at the Oñate Center, which sponsored and housed the statue, had even noticed the amputation. When the newspaper called to confirm, the director had to go out to check that it had really happened. Had no one been notified, the statue would have joined the legion of bronze men on horseback in cities across the world whose names most passers-by can't summon up even as the legacy of their impact continues to be felt. But the severing of statue's foot made visible the contentious legacies of the Spanish footprint on the bodies, backs, and histories of the region.

It was this foot that returned in 2017. One of the surgeon-activists contacted the Cheyenne-Arapaho filmmaker Chris Eyre, telling him that the foot was still in their possession. Eyre arranged clandestine meetings with the "foot thief" for a couple of reporters. We learn from their articles that the appendage is about two feet in length and rather heavy.[27] A photo of the severed foot also appeared in *The New York Times*.[28] It lies on its side atop rumpled black fabric, against earth and scrub, the balls of the foot caught in a stirrup, the bronze toe and ankle aglow in the slanting light while the heel and spur are cast in shadow. It is a foot encased in a boot, of course, the stirrup and spur reminding us that it was the horse's hoof hitting the earth that reinforced the thrust of the conquistador's boot.

26. Trujillo, "Oñate's Foot."
27. Bennett, "After 20 Years."
28. Romero, "It Takes a Foot Thief."

Workers removing the sculpture of Juan de Oñate from the Oñate Center in Alcalde on June 14, 2020. © Eddie Moore. Courtesy: Imago/Zuma Press Wire.

Repair of the statue was quick although there were debates about whether it might not be better to leave the leg amputated. The sculptor was eager to see the statue made whole, lamenting the fact that more people came to see it after the amputation than ever did before.

The furor of the debates around the commemoration eventually subsided, but Oñate has continued to be a symbolic flashpoint. In September 2017, on the occasion of an Entrada pageant in Santa Fe, the statue's left foot was painted red and tagged to remember the 1680 Pueblo Revolt.[29] In the mid-2000s, in Texas, the city of El Paso planned to erect a gigantic thirty-six-foot statue of the conquistador as part of a proposed downtown sculpture-walk through history. City officials had to relocate it to the airport

29. Hummels, "Made Whole Again."

and were forced to rename it, more generically, *The Equestrian*.[30] Nonetheless, that statue did not escape defacement with graffiti and paint during the nationwide protests in 2020 against racism and police brutality. These protests reignited debates about Confederate monuments as well as other statues and symbols in which racist and colonial violence is embedded.[31] In June 2020, the Oñate statue at Alcalde was removed to storage, pending public discussion as to its fate.[32] In 2023, it was announced that the statue would be moved to Española, in front of the sheriff's office, but this was postponed once more in the face of multiple protests.[33] For a statue with an unusual abundance of feet, it seems, for now, that they are up in the air—appropriate indeed for a land in which footprints are about traversals rather than pedestals.

Metaphor/Material

Traces on a border landscape are not the footprint's only treachery. In fact, the footprints that concern people today are equally if not more likely to be carbon footprints, digital footprints, building footprints, or global footprints. The meaning of the footprint has migrated well ahead of the sign of a walker. Journalist and *New York Times* columnist William Safire called it the March of the Metaphoric Footprints. According to him, linguists had traced the origins of this trope to 1965, when it was used to signify "the proposed landing area for a spacecraft."[34] What unites these metaphoric footprints is the overwhelming pressure of their impact and occupation. In fact, as it

---

30. Propp, "A Giant of Ambivalence."
31. Gilbert, "Protests Target Spanish Colonial Statues."
32. Land, "Fate of Alcalde Oñate Statue."
33. Candelaria, "A Ceremony Re-Dedicating an Onate Statue"
34. Safire, "Footprint."

marches forward, the footprint seems to be less capacious a term than consumptive. It takes up space rather than travels across it.

Among the early metaphors was the ecological footprint coined in the 1990s by ecological economist, William Rees, and his then doctoral student, Mathis Wackernagel. It measures the natural resources required for any single activity in order to calculate the impact of humans on the world. On one side is demand—the total ecological assets such as plant foods, livestock, fish, and timber needed to produce the natural resources consumed by a population as well as to absorb its waste, especially carbon emissions. On the other is supply—the availability of productive resources such as cropland, grazing land, fishing grounds, built-up land, forest cover, and carbon demand on land. The ecological footprint assesses the land and water required to sustain a population and a material standard indefinitely. The sum total of ecological footprints of human populations is the human footprint on the planet.[35]

Even as a metaphor, the ecological footprint retained its human scale and some of the physical and phenomenological attributes of a footprint such as weight, pressure, and impact on the ground—it was characterized as a measure of the "load" of a given human population on natural resources. When Rees and Wackernagel first tried to describe the concept, they took their readers on a walk around what they called a "fair earthshare" to show them what it might feel like to inhabit a finite world—a leisurely walk around one's fair share of the earth would apparently take only ten minutes. Their footprint is spatial: measure a hectare and mark it with flags, they suggest, and then see how long it takes to walk

---

35. Wackernagel and Rees, *Our Ecological Footprint*.

around it. Or imagine you're standing in the center of a square field that represents an average earthshare; you'll find you can see the boundary less than seventy-five meters away.[36] Earthshares are not distributed equitably, so some people can and will hardly move while others blithely stamp across the world. In fact, by their reckoning, if everyone on the planet lived like an average North American, we would need three Earths to live sustainably.[37]

The ecological footprint has largely been overtaken by the carbon footprint, which measures the total amount of carbon dioxide or other carbon compounds emitted as a result of the consumption of fossil fuels by the activity of any entity. Decoupled from the ecological footprint's connection to land (and water), the carbon footprint is not tied to place. Nor is it tied only to human or animal bodies. Rees and Wackernagel did allow that such diverse items as tomatoes and bridges could have ecological footprints based not only on the resources that were used to create or transport them but also indirectly in terms of the kinds of lifestyles they would enable. The carbon footprint is even more transcendent—everything has a footprint—and it is less spatial. Although it conveys a general sense of impact, this does not appear as a visible or tangible effect in space or on a surface.

Still, its attraction seems due, at least in part, to the agency it appears to give individuals in its calculation. This agency has a perverse origin. The phrase was popularized by a campaign designed by advertising and public relations agency Ogilvy and Mather between 2004 and 2006 for the oil and gas company BP. It sought to divert attention from the impact on the climate crisis of BP's fossil fuel ex-

36. Pasek, "Fixing Carbon," 108.
37. Wackernagel and Rees, op. cit.

traction by shifting focus to individual responsibility.[38] This was not a novel strategy—researchers analyzing the public and internal documents of ExxonMobil have demonstrated how the company has systematically shifted responsibility for climate change from itself onto consumers while presenting reliance on fossil fuels as necessary and inevitable.[39] Within two years of the BP campaign, "carbon footprint" was the *Oxford English Dictionary*'s U.K. word of the year and, since then, it has seeped into everyday consciousness as a series of injunctions and prescriptions for individual daily life that will somehow stay the gargantuan forces of corporate action. Even as these corporations continue with business as usual or engage in emissions trading with carbon credits and offsets, many anxious and conscientious people keep track of the carbon footprints of their own activities and try to reduce or mitigate them. It doesn't require a very lengthy internet search to bring up some sort of carbon footprint calculator.

This nervous on-line self-examination spills its own crumbs, adding to a trail of cookies and other data from overall internet activity that creates a digital footprint for each person on the web. The life span of digital footprints rivals their lunar kin—as long as the cloud exists, the footprints of our virtual adventures and misadventures will remain. These footprints, whether passive—that is, inadvertently furnished—or active—for instance, on social media— have come to stand in for the identities of people themselves. Data mining and the algorithms generated on the basis of our footprints create virtual shadows that can become more significant than their human originals—consider the effect of an on-line indiscretion on future employment or, worse still, relent-

---

38. Solman, "BP: Coloring Public Opinion?"
39. Supran and Oreskes, "Rhetoric and Frame Analysis of ExxonMobil's Climate Change Communications."

less surveillance by indefatigable electronic monitoring systems, ostensibly for security purposes.

All metaphoric footprints retain a troubled and curious relationship to the individual, placing as they do the burden of extractive histories and technologies on the uplifted arch and forward toe of a human foot. But what are we to do now that the lithe and curious material trace has given way to the weighty and anxious metaphor? The footprint has never been entirely innocent, of course; it has always been an object of contradictory forensics. The footprints of the early striding hominins in African ash release ancestral energies of movement, companionship, courage, and curiosity just as those of Aldrin and Armstrong on the moon evoke wonder, imagination, and exploration. But each of those steps carries with it the histories of human occupation, imperialism, territoriality, and impact, a legacy of treading upon others as much as treading on the world.

As the footprint grows stouter, heavier, and more rigid, its monumentality invites desecration and defacement. Has the term become too loose and wayward to salvage any political promise? Or does the inherently enigmatic character of the footprint militate against too swift a foreclosure of imagination? What if we resisted the temptation to dismiss the footprint as much too messy a concept but instead took it up as an invitation to work through contradictions without reconciliation? We can look to other itineraries, other lineages of the term, other material manifestations wherein the footprint is light not leaden. We could return to simple mechanics, which demonstrate that a footprint is formed by the foot pressing into the ground *and leaving it*. A footprint is inherently mobile, not static. No foot leaves a trace if it doesn't rise. The print of the foot demands its absence. It is a paradox that the footprint must risk if it is to survive.

Making/Taking

In a time before this time, says the ancient Sanskrit text *Bhagavata Purana*, the cosmic order was in upheaval.[40] When the mighty king Mahabali extended his sway over all the worlds, the power of the gods waned. As the king performed a sacrificial ceremony, a mendicant dwarf approached the ritual area. At such an auspicious time, no request could be declined, so Mahabali was prepared to offer alms and generously so. But the little man declined his largesse, asking only for three paces of land. The request was modest, even laughable, coming as it did from this diminutive man, and the king granted his wish. "Stop," counselled the king's mentor, discerning that there was more at stake here than met the eye. Yet now that the wish had been granted, the king wouldn't retract his word, even if he was in jeopardy. Smiling, the dwarf took his first step, and with it he covered the earth, for he was none other than the god Vishnu in another incarnation. His second step filled the skies. Where shall I place the third? he asked. The devout Mahabali, duly chastened, bowed his head to receive the divine foot that would push him to the underworld. Thus does a lowly footprint assert its unassailable power.

On its face, this is a lesson in humility. The dwarf avatar brings hubris down to earth and restores a cosmic equilibrium. But other interpretations are subtler. Even as the king grants the request and the dwarf takes the first two steps, a lie is exposed: The earth was not Mahabali's to give, nor could he possess the heavens. The arrogance that believes in its ownership and possession must surrender in the face of the truth. But wait, the story doesn't end there either, because Vishnu's intervention itself is not without guile. Mahabali was a just ruler, beloved of his people, but he was

40. Subramaniam, *Srimad Bhagavatam*.

In the center, Vishnu's *trivikrama* or three strides; to the left, Queen Kaikeyi reminds King Dasharatha of Mahabali's sacrifice. Rajasthan, India, c. 1710. Gum tempera, ink, and gold on paper. Creative Commons (CC0) license, original image at The Cleveland Museum of Art.

an *asura*, a class of demigods opposed to another group of divine beings called the *deva*s. His dominance had roused their jealousy. Vishnu had acquiesced to the devas' pleas for intercession and was working his cunning to secure their success—it was this stratagem that Mahabali's mentor discerned when he cautioned the king. Was this act of divine duplicity a mythic depiction of very real histories—the suppression of local populations as new settlers from the northwest entered the Indian peninsula around 1500 BCE? Some think so, seeing in the demonization of asuras and other anti-gods, often depicted as dark, lusty, and power-hungry beings, the deep-seated strain of casteist ideologies that continue into the present. Once more, the evidence the footprint offers in the dwarf avatar is ambiguous, as divine domination appears to supplant the foot's pedagogic touch. But the suppression of Vishnu's foot is not unleavened. Mahabali was not relegated to permanent darkness, so that in some traditions he reappears annually before his people at harvesttime to much celebration and fanfare.

There is an even earlier conception of the three strides of Vishnu that predates its appearance in the story of Mahabali and the dwarf. In this telling, with his first step, Vishnu covers the earth—in doing so, he creates it, making room for all who dwell here. With his second he makes the sky—the air, ether, space—and with his third he goes beyond our vision to where the god himself dwells. We cannot see this last divine step, but the earth and skies with our sun and moon are visible, and what we do with that vision is up to us. These three mythic strides suggest that every step is a creative act that brings a world into being. Each step we take must make space for others. A footstep that makes rather than takes is the one that leaves a footprint. A true footprint then cedes ground to those who come after.

ITINERARY 2

PACE

In Step and Out of Step

At midnight on December 31, 2022, the United States retired a foot. The difference between its two feet was tiny—one hundredth of a foot—and scarcely perceptible to the eye, but when it came to vast distances or the computing of coordinates, the difference could be significant enough, suggests the National Oceanic and Atmospheric Administration (NOAA), to move someone in Virginia over the border to Kentucky.[1] The foot being retired was the U.S. survey foot, older and longer than its companion, the international foot. Both feet were a result of calibration against the meter, but at different times—the survey foot in 1893, and the international foot in 1959—resulting in two more or less equivalent feet used variably by different states, different agencies, and for different purposes—the international foot deployed for precision engineering and the U.S. survey foot for coordinate mapping and measurement. This curious example of U.S. federalism has man-

1. NOAA, "A Tale of Two Feet." See video.

aged to exist despite the inevitable confusions that have arisen for those walking past each other's feet.

As the National Geodetic Survey (NGS) was already recalibrating the coordinates of the National Spatial Reference System, which determines where the United States exists on the globe, it was an opportune time to kick off on the right foot—in fact, that was among the kinds of metaphors of this change, along with "putting the best foot forward" or "a step in the right direction." But it didn't come easily. A major rub lay in the names—the *U.S.* survey foot was giving way to the *international* foot. Timothy W. Burch of the National Society of Professional Surveyors said to *The New York Times*, "For unfortunately a lot of Americans, especially in this day and age, anything that has to do with the U.S. and that naming quality being taken away, it's like we're under attack. So there is a portion of the country that's like, No, this is ours, this is what we're going to keep."[2]

The term "foot" had lodged itself in an imagination bounded by nation and culture. From the outset for some, the meter was an interloper. In 1866, soon after the U.S. authorized the use of the metric system, a university panel was appointed at the erstwhile Columbia College in New York with a view to establishing its merits. The senior mathematician chairing the panel did the opposite, finding the meter defective, not only decrying metric measurement generally but lamenting the loss of "short, sharp Saxon words" if the country ceded to the Latinate decameter and centimeter.[3] In a presentation to a society of civil engineers in 2021, Michael Dennis, a geodesist from the NGS and a proponent of the change, allowed that the international foot had a whiff of so-

---

2. Mitchell, "America Has Two Feet."
3. De Simone and Treat, "A History of the Metric System Controversy," 52.

cialism and "New World Order" about it while the U.S. survey foot seemed more patriotic. However, he assured the Texas-based audience, their already large state would be gaining eight more feet through this change.[4] Truth be told, measurement has always been the stuff of politics.

The now solo foot is to be simply called "the foot" from here on out, said the NGS, although surveyors will have to deal with some legacy applications of the nomenclature to the U.S. survey foot.[5] This deprecation, as it is called, of the survey foot, is not because the international foot is more accurate; it is primarily to standardize measurement across the country. Whether the *pied du roi* of the Ancien Regime or the king's foot, attributed to Henry I of England, the establishment of weights and measures has long been a sovereign right. What the measures correspond to is a more open matter—the English and French feet varied in length—but it remains the case that governments are keen to establish absolute authority over the weights and measures used in their territories. Almost immediately after settling questions of economy and defense in his young administration, George Washington, once a surveyor himself, was keen to establish standardized weights and measures. Each of the two feet in the United States came into being through an act of Congress.

The meter, now a widely used global measure, was originally proposed by France as a universal system of measurement. Birthed in the Enlightenment spirit of rationality and progress and amid growing revolutionary fervor, the ambition of the meter

4. Dennis, "The Measure of All Things after 2022." The same webinar slide deck, without the Texas inflection, is available on the NGS website.
5. National Institute of Standards and Technology, "U.S. Survey Foot."

was that it would be a measure for everyone because it was derived from the earth rather than a human body, albeit a royal one. The new measurement was determined as one ten-millionth of the distance from the Equator to the North Pole. It was seen as being for all people, for all time, by French philosopher Condorcet. "Not from history or the fiat of kings," but from nature.[6] No longer would measures be derived from human labor or the human body but from something beyond the human which might be said to be held in common. It was infused with the principles of the time—rational, coherent, and egalitarian. Measuring, however, is a human action even if grafted on to the planet. Establishing the meter required getting back on the road on one's feet—or in a carriage.

The meridian that would be used to triangulate the measurements was the one that ran from Dunkerque to Barcelona through Paris. Two *savants*, Jean Baptiste Joseph Delambre and Pierre Francois André Méchain, set out from Paris, each travelling in the opposite direction. They were both astronomers, Méchain older and melancholic, Delambre inordinately calm and dedicated, and their remarkable seven-year project (1792–1799) was carried out amid the political turmoil of the French Revolution. Ill-paid though they were, they remained determined, negotiating with various political factions to be allowed to continue their journeys or with villagers to build towers or additions to church steeples to conduct their observations and measurements. Their tireless triangulations were the basis for the first definition of the

---

6. This account of measuring the meter is derived substantially from Alder, *The Measure of All Things*.

meter, which was then produced into an actual physical standard, a prototype platinum meter bar held in Paris, later expanded to several platinum-iridium bars held across the globe. The definition of the meter itself has undergone many changes since then, related to the wavelength of krypton-86 and of light in a vacuum, among other standards, with each re-definition aiming for greater abstraction and scientific accuracy.

In retiring the U.S. survey foot, Brett Howe, the geodetic services division chief at NGS, stated: "Our vision at NOAA's National Geodetic Survey is that everyone accurately knows where they are and where other things are at all times and in all places."[7] But it's precisely because people thought they knew where they were that there was ever any dissension about the adoption of the meter over the foot. The U.S. had been interested in the French proposition until the choice of meridian was revealed. Thomas Jefferson, a supporter who, during his French sojourn, had befriended Condorcet, was miffed at what he saw as a parochial choice rather than the one in which the United States would have a presence.

The British wondered the same: why should a standard founded on the quadrant of the earth's circumference passing through the meridian of Paris be a better one than ours, asked a Member of Parliament in 1868. Were Englishmen and Englishwomen to be driven out of their customs and into the adoption of a foreign nomenclature, put another honorable member to the assembly, while a third concluded that "there was quite enough labour in running the race of life, without carrying lead in one's shoes."[8] Parliamentary hansards on metrication over the years reveal on-

---

7. NOAA, "A Tale of Two Feet."
8. Hansards may be found at https://hansard.parliament.uk

going debates about the scientific merits and trade advantages as well as the impact of these changes on the British way of life. In fact, the U.K. did not take the plunge until 1965 when it was considering entry into the European Common Market, although in 1975 there were still complaints of "dragging our feet." By that time, the kind of argument that had once prevailed—that they would enjoy an advantage over competitors on the continent because of their colonial possessions where the British foot and other weights and measures had been adopted—was no longer tenable. The empire had ended, and the imperial system's days were numbered. By this time, the U.S. had calibrated its foot against the meter, meaning that U.S. and British feet would also diverge despite their common name. Yet as late as 1980, the first chair of the U.K.'s Metrication Board underscored for parliamentarians, "One cannot go to the moon in feet per minute," adding "the world cannot be entirely out of step and we cannot be the only ones in step."

Whatever the nomenclature and no matter how abstracted from the human, weights and measures are often translated into and felt in the body. In June 2020, the New York City subways began to sport bright yellow decals of footprints to indicate the six feet that the Centers for Disease Control (CDC) had announced was the necessary distance to maintain between people to stem the spread of the Covid-19 virus. The MTA's (Metropolitan Transit Authority) campaign launched with considerable humor and inclusivity, as the decals showed pawprints, hoofprints, high heels, as well as sneakers and wheelchair prints. The CDC's mandate enshrined in most bodies in the U.S. a perceptible sense of a six-foot distance just as the WHO recommendation of one or two meters adopted in parts of the world seeped into other bones.

Social distancing decals in the New York City subways. Photograph: Author, July 2020.

The awkwardly phrased "social distancing" was a reminder that measurement is indeed as social as it is technical.

As the meter moved away from Méchain's and Delambre's feet, beyond physical standards into scientific determinations related to the length travelled by light in a vacuum in a specific time frame, it has held on to the ideology of universal sovereignty. It's nobody's foot. And being replicable anywhere under laboratory conditions, it makes international cooperation and comprehension possible. However, the legacy of anthropometric measure has remained not just in measurement vocabularies but in the transformation of the deprecated limb into an image of anthropogenic impact.

The power of carbon and ecological footprints as metaphors and mental images rests in no small part on the residue of measurement we recognize in them. The footprint is more than a generalized pressure, it's a measurable one. The original impetus for the meter was to find a planetary standard that would transcend local decree, yet we are asked to reckon with human impact on the planet in the metaphors of measurement we have supposedly forsworn. In any case, footprints around the planet are not the same. Older localized measures could register the incommensurability between the agricultural potential of two different parcels of land or the time it takes to walk somewhere in mountainous terrain versus the plains. Having lost the inherent variation and difference of measurement, all countries are held to the same metric, no matter their histories or levels of industrialization, urbanization, extraction, and development, which has scuppered more than one effort at international cooperation around global warming and carbon emissions.

Atlas and Abstraction

Méchain's and Delambre's travels along the meridian had a predecessor in the Cassini mapping project, commissioned in the 1660s by the newly established French Academy of Sciences and conducted by four generations of one family over six decades. The Cassinis were astronomers, cartographers, and scientists of Italian origin. The last of the generations responsible for the project, Cassini IV as he was called, was a candidate for the meter measurement program since his father, grandfather, and great grandfather each had, in his time, surveyed the meridian that passed through Paris. The first of the Cassinis, a keen observer of the solar system, is also known for a detailed map of the moon, in which he placed the face of a woman at the apex of one of its capes. She appears to be his wife, so that Cassini I's insertion, almost 300 years before Apollo 11, is an early human imprint, albeit that of a lover's heart, on the lunar surface.[9] The Academy's commission, however, was a down-to-earth affair.

Directed from Paris by the family, a vast array of surveyors was dispatched across France to conduct the triangulations, which they could not do without the cooperation of provincial leaders, priests, and farmers, who not only granted permission but often, particularly in the case of residents, had better knowledge of the terrain. Inhabitants would sometimes object to the focus on chateaux and churches, which were considered relatively stable sites for triangulation purposes, to the exclusion of other features like paths and streams, which they held to be more important. It was the first systematic survey of the realm based on triangulation—and realm it still was in pre-Revolutionary France, even though the maps were to be appropriated into a revolutionary national imaginary by the late eighteenth century. The result was a series of detailed topographic plates, totaling thirty-six square feet.

Medieval maps tended to be itinerary maps that were about routes people took.[10] They were not necessarily to scale, often sketchy, focused on the places one encountered and often more textual. The maps were linear and temporal rather than geometric, and contained the relevant information required by the traveler rather than measures of distance. Travel was still a felt experience rather than an

9. Godlewska, "Geography and Cassini IV." The lunar map with Cassini I's moon maiden gazing toward the shape of a heart in the lunar sea may be viewed on the Paris Observatory's website.

10. The characterization of medieval mapping draws from Branch, *The Cartographic State*, and Turnbull, "Cartography and Science in Early Modern Europe."

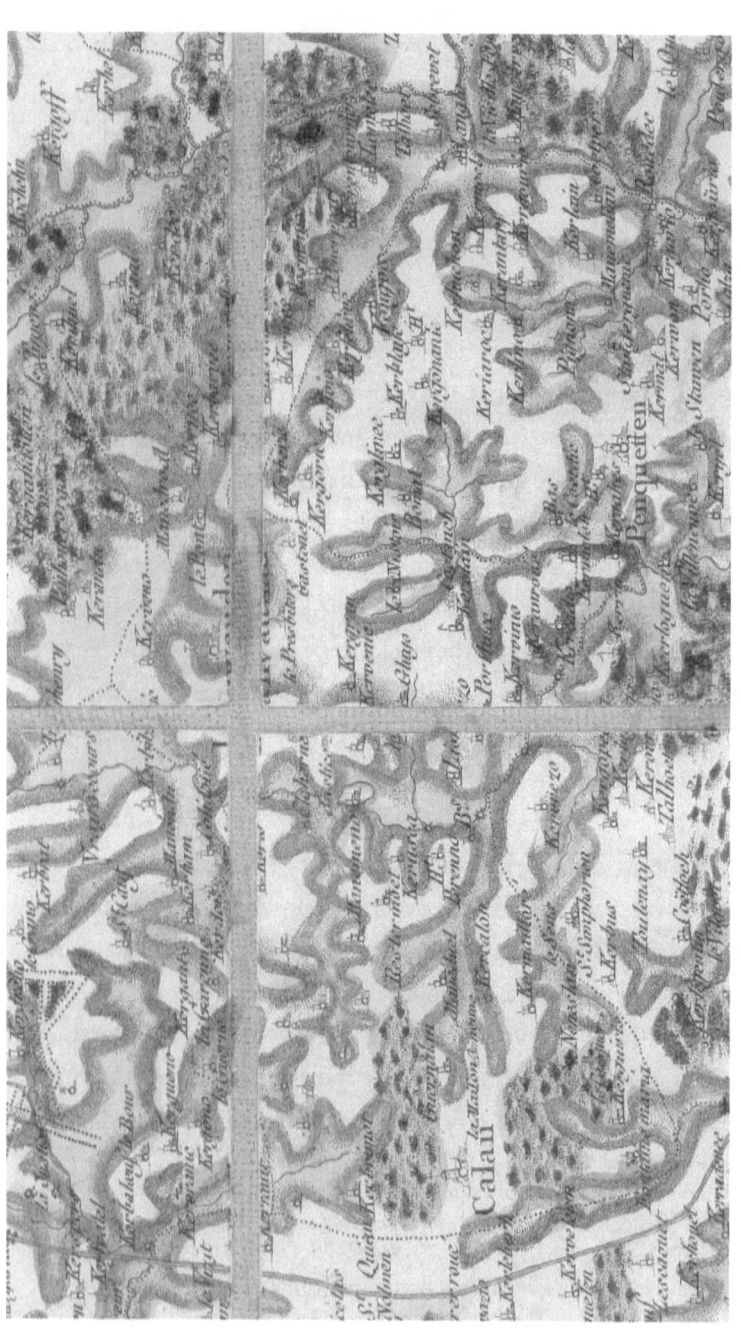

Section of the Cassini Map. César-François Cassini de Thury (Cassini III), 1789. Public domain, via Wikimedia Commons.

abstracted set of coordinates that were not always adaptable to the body. Power issued from the ruler, but it radiated outward in a series of feudal relationships to ambiguous peripheries. Fuzzy boundaries where there might be overlaps, enclaves, and disputes were tolerated as long as the feudal chain from lords to sovereign was relatively clear. Kings didn't commission maps; when needed, they used commercial ones produced by traders and sailors, which then provided them with an image of sorts of the lands under their sway.

Mapmaking became more active in Europe from the fifteenth century onward, with the rediscovery of Ptolemy's *Geography* and as Europeans began to travel to places hitherto unknown to them. The Ptolemaic graticule—a grid system of latitude and longitude—in relation to heavenly coordinates was intended to locate places accurately on Earth. Astronomy and geography went hand in hand. No more fuzzy boundaries and loose collections of places and people; the world could be plotted with increasing precision as techniques of projection and triangulation contributed to a more scientific cartography. Places gave way to space, all too frequently the blanked terra incognita of the so-called explorer, that could be delineated through triangulation, grids, and lines. The map was an image, suggests Jordan Branch, and borders were now clear lines. Cassini's map, even with its beautifully drawn individual plates showing clumps of trees, shaded hills, and rivers, produces an overall image of France that is familiar to our eyes today. The revolutionaries saw it. They seized the maps and papers, took them to the War Depot, finally making them publicly available to the new citizens of the nation-state as a collective image of their *patrie*.

The British, with a wary eye on the French and attentive to their own imperial ambitions, were supported by colonial trading companies in cartographic projects using the new triangulation technologies. The Great Trigonometrical Survey (GTS) of India was launched in 1802 to survey the sub-continent. It started in the south but by the mid-nineteenth century had reached the Himalayas. Maps were as strategic as they were informational. The British were keen to establish precise frontiers as well as gain geographical, military, and political knowledge regarding their neighbors. Natural barriers such as mountains and the watersheds of rivers were often seen as potentially scientific demarcations of strategic concerns. By the 1860s, however, Tibet was closed to Europeans and there were also incidents of hostility against them in other parts of Central Asia so that it became increasingly harder for the British to leave the safety of their territories.

It was at this juncture that Captain Montgomerie of the Royal Engineers, who was working with the GTS, proposed the recruitment of Indians to undertake survey work. It was not utterly unheard of, since Indians had been involved in earlier projects in the eighteenth century, but the practice had waned because the British grew concerned that Indians would acquire technical expertise and geographical knowledge of sensitive frontier regions. However, given that the only people crossing borders freely and regularly were Indians, no choice lay ahead but to hire them. The first of these hires, the results of whose measurement by pacing was evaluated against existing British surveys, proved to be remarkably accurate, thereby inaugurating an entire system of stealth mapping. Extraordinary geographical and cultural knowledge was generated about Himalayan territories, the Indus and Sutlej watersheds and more by the *pundits* (as they were collectively called, after the most notable of them, Nain Singh Rawat, whose schoolmaster title it was).[11]

11. Waller, *The Pundits* provides a full account of the role of these men. Detailed reports were also given by Captains Montgomerie and Trotter to the

The pundits did not move using their natural stride but were trained to walk a fixed pace and maintain it regardless of terrain. They were drilled on the parade ground in Dehradun until they could walk 2,000 paces at a 31.5-inch step to equal a mile. They also learned the use of a sextant, how to recognize stars, use a boiling point thermometer and a prismatic compass with Hindi or Persian numerals, and take notes. Frequently disguised as lamas and Buddhist pilgrims, they were issued rosaries with a hundred beads (instead of the customary Buddhist one hundred and eight) to keep track of their counts. Each small bead signified a hundred paces while every tenth bead was a larger *rudraksha* seed, signifying 1,000. Tibetan prayer wheels provided further disguise and could be used to secrete strips of paper with measurement information. The British withheld astronomical tables or instruction in route survey calculations so the Indians would not "falsify data" and lauded it as "native enterprise directed by English intelligence," but there was no doubt in anyone's mind that the work of these men was invaluable.[12] Colonel Henry Yule, who advocated for awarding Nain Singh Rawat the Royal Geographical Society's gold medal (over Montgomerie's successor, Capt. Trotter), said the pundit was no "topographical automaton" but responsible for adding more to the knowledge of Asia than any living person.[13]

Nain Singh kept a diary.[14] Only occasionally alluding to his pac-

---

Royal Geographical Society (RGS). A letter from Col. Edmund Smyth recounting his memories of Nain Singh Rawat was also published as an obituary by the RGS.
12. Waller, *The Pundits*, Chapter 2.
13. Waller, *The Pundits*, Chapter 4, Sec. Nain Singh's Last Exploration.
14. Pangtey, *Saga of a Native Explorer*.

तारीख १४ फेबरी सन् १८७३ ई० केरोज़ ज़नाब मेज़र मन्टगामरी साहिब बहादुर डी० डी०
सुपरेन्टेन्डेन्ट जी० टी० सर्वे मुक़ामदेहरे में मुझे हुक्म हुआ कि पंडित नैनसिंह दरियाय ब्रह्मपुत्र का पुरा गर
याफ़्त करने का जाय॰ चुनांचे कोह॰ अल्मोडेस इलाहाबाद साहिबगंज तक रेलगाड़ी से वहां से काह्म गर
लिङ व शिकिम होकर ग्याद्चे को निकले वहां से ल्हासा के मुत्तसिल च्याकममे श्वाड़ी वह्झुस्युल नाह्म
                  कत्ताहूआ
नहसे दरियाय ब्रह्मपुत्र के किनारे २ पेमायश ल्हाग्चौंली होकर लसनपूर सरकारी अहल्दारी तक
मकरे

बमूजिब हुक्म साहिब मोम्फ़िके ता॰ १५ फेबरी के रोज़ मन्देहरे में कूच किया रेलगाड़ी महज़न
से मुरादाबाद तक वहां से सराकर अल्मोड़ा में पहुंचा॰ अल्मोड़ा में सफ़र दरियाय ब्रह्मपुत्र बाब्त
नोकर बग़ैरह का बन्दोबस्त जैसा मुनासिब था किया पर ओज़ार देहरे में मेरे पास न पहुंचने के सबब
कईरोज़ ओज़ारों के इंतिज़ारी पर बैठना पड़ा इसबीच १ चिट्ठा हुक्मनामा जनाब हेन्सी साहिब
बहादुर डिप्टी सुपरंटंडंट का इस मज़मून से० मेरे नाम सादिर हूआ कि जवतक कर्नेल वाक्रसाहिब
बहादुर से दूसरा हुक्म तुम्हार सफ़र के निस्बत न आवे तवतक तुम सफ़र में न जाना ————

ता॰ २६ फेबरी के रोज़ ओज़ार भी मस्रफ़ित क्मा के पहुंच गया ० दूमरे हुक्म ओनेसी
इंतजारी पर कईरोज़ गुज़र गये बाद ता॰ ५ एप्रेल ७३ केरोज़ जनाब हेन्सी साहिब बहादुर
डिप्टी सुपरंटंडंट से दूसरा हुक्म युं सादिर हूआ कि अन्दर गहिल्ने हुक्म को मनसुर

Nain Singh's entry for 14 February 1873, Yarkand-Khotan Diary, outlining the order from Major Montgomerie to explore the course of the Brahmaputra River. Courtesy Shekhar Pathak/PAHAR Collection, Nainital.

ing, it is an unadorned account of his travels and observations of places and people, through ill health and personal danger, over bleak terrain made harsher at times by the necessity to maintain secrecy. Imagine the man walking. The coordination of hand, foot, and mind in a meditative multitasking, balancing the need to be alert to his surroundings with the need to keep count, pacing evenly, repeating and recording such that his footprints would ultimately transform into boundary lines and thereby obliterate the work of his feet. Nain Singh walked 1,200 miles, measuring 2.5 million paces over two and a half years. The numbers make one gasp; their exactitude is compelling. Nain Singh's cousin, Kishen Singh (codename A.K.), during his own mapping expedition, found himself stuck in Dunhuang because of the local governor's suspicions. Sick, lonely, and nervous, he left with a lama as soon as he was better. But the lama was afraid of being robbed and wouldn't countenance going on foot, which was necessary for pacing; he insisted on traveling horseback. Unfazed, Kishen Singh estimated the length of the horse's stride and counted the number of times the right foreleg hit the ground. Foot and hoof in partnership mapped the high Himalayas.

While Indians were turned into what Kapil Raj has memorably called "human instruments" and the tramping of French citizen-subject surveyors was transformed into topographical lines, the Spanish colonial cartographic enterprise provoked unexpected insertions.[15] In 1578, Juan López de Velasco, appointed Chief Cosmographer-Chronicler of the Indies by Philip II, who was eager to have a map of his New World territories, sent out a 50-item questionnaire to New Spain to help him prepare one.[16] This was one of the long-distance fact-finding and determinative Relaciones Geográficas efforts. Items 10, 42, and 47 made a request for maps. The questionnaire asked that local inhabitants be consulted for the textual answers, but it wasn't assumed they would write them. It's likely that López de Velasco thought that the maps too would be produced in a similar way. However, the colonists gave that over to the *indios*, who were regarded as the image-makers because of their logographic and pictographic writing, which

15. Raj, "When Human Travellers Become Instruments."
16. The account of Meso-American mapping and response to the Relaciones Geográficas relies on the following: Herren Rajagopalan, *Portraying the Aztec Past*; Hidalgo, *Trail of Footprints*; Mundy, *The Mapping of New Spain*; Navarrete, "The Path from Aztlan to Mexico."

stood in contrast to "literate" alphabetic Spanish. Some colonists produced itinerary-style maps, but the questionnaire asked for a *pintura*, and that was a task for an indigenous painter.

The worldview that gave the *tlacuiloque* or artist-scribes their visual grammar had been shattered by the Spanish but some of its practices still left their footprints—literally so. In 1580, Pedro de San Agustín was commissioned by Fernando de Oñate, brother of the New Mexico conquistador Juan de Oñate, to create a pintura of Culhuacan. Now a neighborhood in southern Mexico City, historically Culhuacan was a major administrative center, which was at that point within the jurisdiction of Don Fernando. In the center of the pintura is the glyph identifying Culhuacan, in keeping with traditional indigenous practice of identifying places with logographs. Churches and other buildings are labelled in Spanish and the map depicts rivers, mountains, and trees. Studded on the roadways and paths into, through, and at the bottom of the image are footprints. They are not graphic symbols, like the walker sign at a zebra crossing whose stance is unrelated to the direction of pedestrian traffic. Right and left foot alternate in the map; these feet are moving and in specific directions.

Before the Conquest, it would have been critical to establish how a people came to inhabit a place, the narrative of their migration a story commencing at their origins and depicting their arrival in a new homeland. It was their journey from Aztlán to the region of today's Mexico City that established who the Culhua-Mexica were, for instance, and that granted them not only their relationship to the land but also their authority—even their right to rule, which they did as the magnificent imperial Aztecs, as the Europeans were to call them. Oral histories continued to be recounted even after the Spanish arrived, with the tlacuiloque

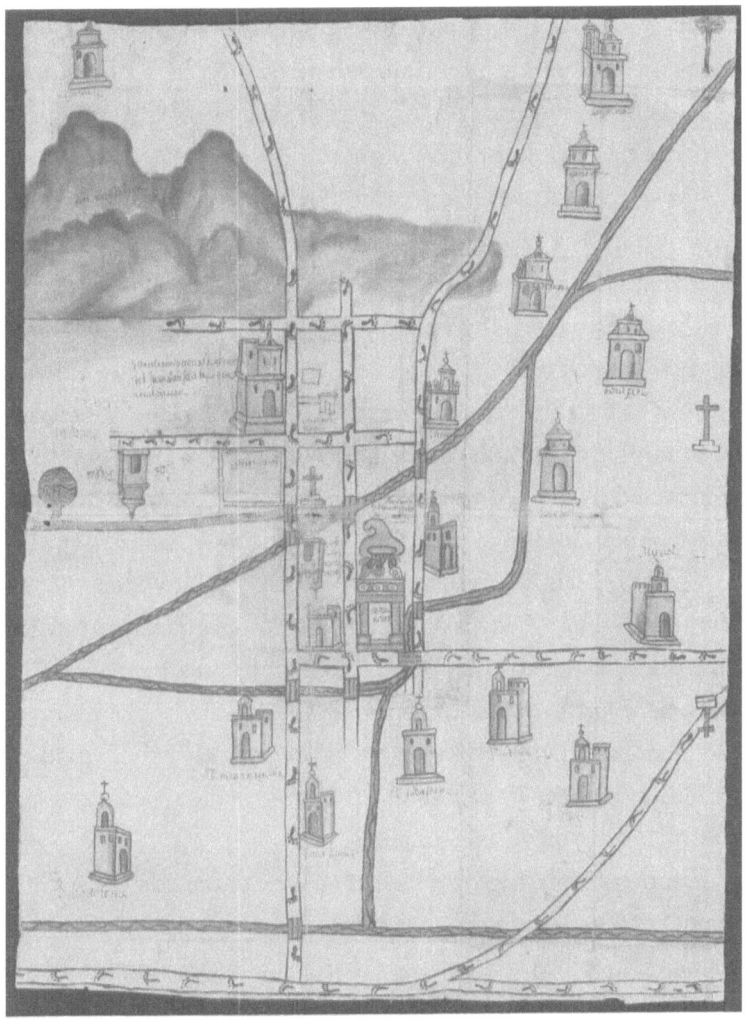

Pintura de Culhuacan, 1580. Credit: Benson Latin American Collection, LLILAS Benson Latin American Studies and Collections, The University of Texas at Austin.

creating the painted manuscripts to go with them. Traditional narratives wrapped time and space together and the footprint was one way to demonstrate this on maps, which always situated places connected by footprints within a calendar of days. Footprints would start near a year sign, indicating the year that the Mexica departed from a place, and continue until they reached another place sign, the next stopping point in the migration.

These feet signify motion rather than occupation, functioning not as images of the past but of actions taken in time. Space did not exist as an abstraction; it was made by human actions of walking and naming. In some instances, footprints were accompanied by hoofprints, in recognition of the Spanish presence that had brought in horses, sheep, oxen and other animals to this new world. Nahuatl reckoning of distance was in terms of the rest required by a body en route just as European medieval mapping once reckoned with the needs of a body on a journey. In the same way, localized measures in Europe and elsewhere reflected the labor required to till a field of one crop rather than another, or indicated what its soil might produce, rendering nonsensical equivalents based on acreage alone.

Painting was a high-status indigenous profession. Therefore, many of the tlacuiloque responding to the questionnaires had trained in monastic schools. This had made them aware of Western iconography (the monks pressed them into painting church cloths) but they were also exposed to Aztec and Mixtec painted manuscripts, kept in storerooms, that taught them indigenous mapping conventions and symbols. The paper and ink were provided by the church but the map-drawings these painters made were based on their own traditions of community-mapping rather than the drawing of cities and topography. By the late sixteenth century, these painters had also adapted this mapping to make community records that could be used for petitions in land disputes. The boundaries on many maps were lined with footprints to mark the ritual of boundary walking that historically demarcated places. Community members walked to mark territories but also to integrate into their bodies the experience and knowledge of place. The footprints memorialized a repeated but ephemeral act. Footprints also frequently appeared on roads, in a variety of shapes that Alex Hidalgo suggests are an unofficial signature of the artist.

These indigenous maps insert the foot that has always been part of the mapping process but which modern cartography has sought to remove. They remind us of the journey where the map is content with the road. They insist on recognizing mobility, even uncertainty, when it is desired that matters are settled. The line on modern maps not only records what is permanent, not transitory or in flux, it also produces that permanence whether in the route of a river or the erasure of complex borderlands. We can see in the straight lines of several U.S. state boundaries, along the parallels, the feet of the surveyors. They indicate that the boundaries were not created by the bends of a river or staked along other natural or agreed-upon barriers but deliberately drawn. Surveyors with ax-men cut the woodland to make it possible to measure directly along the latitude. In those straight lines is the history of that felling, the disappearance of American forests and with it, other lives, other species, and their epistemologies. Colonial footprints depended on being able to extend across distances without the foot, mapping unknown areas through techniques and measurements designated as universal. As territories became clearer on a map, so did the rationale for grasping them and the compulsion to do so. Once the cartographic image had taken hold in the mind, it obviated the need to recognize other footprints on the land, even blinded one to them.

Fitting Cinderella

Anyone who has stepped into a shoe knows what it means to adapt one's body to standardized measurement. Will its generic shape adjust to receive one's bones and calluses, how long might it take to break it in, and aah, the pleasure of finally slipping into well-worn footwear. The word "last," a mechanical form in the shape of a foot that shoemakers and cobblers use to make and repair shoes, traces its origins to the Old English footprint. Feet quest for the ideal shoe but shoes often turn the tables, demanding that feet conform to them. Feet that perfectly fit a shoe have long been moments of miraculous revelation, as in the tale of Cinderella or her Chinese equivalent, Ye Xian, or the many global variants of the story. Women's feet have borne the greater mythic burden of an expectation to captivate men through a performance of exact measurement.

In 1999, the Zhiqiang Shoe Factory in Harbin halted production of "lotus shoes," the three-inch shoes that catered to a diminishing clientele of women with bound feet. In her illuminating account of the practice, Dorothy Ko describes the ways in which discourses around the beauty of a foot fixated on its size and measurement.[17] The expression "foot binding" encapsulates a widely variant set of practices that established the ongoing shaping by a woman of her feet, which in turn shaped her. Between the thirteenth and nineteenth centuries, this practice was a singular and

---

17. Ko, *Cinderella's Sisters*. See also, *Every Step a Lotus*.

ongoing experience in the lives of women in China. Along with the control and care of their feet, shoemaking in general was women's work. They did not use the wooden lasts that the Harbin factory employed but made shoes out of cloth, usually silk and cotton textiles, weaving, spinning, cutting patterns, embroidering and mending, even cultivating silkworms for the purpose.

Most of us have lost access to this handcrafted relationship between footwear and feet and the kinds of prints left by their soles. The mass-produced sandals, boots and shoes in which we test the comfort of our feet resolutely resist the imprint of both maker and user. There is no residue of the hands that made them and no proposition about the feet they were made for. Where the perfect fit of Cinderella or Ye Xian prompts the delight of identification, the shoe of today converts unique measurements to a generalized size into which many can and must fit. Each person tries to make sense of numerical sizes, half-sizes, and their international equivalents, and navigates the thicket of wides and regulars in different brands to enhance the comfort, beauty, and mobility of their own feet. But the global shoe esperanto that underlies the crisscross of massive commodity chains is made possible by the language of specific feet.

In his fascinating ethnography of the global shoe industry, Claudio Benzecry describes the work of women fit models whose position and expertise in the chains of production produces the globalized shoe.[18] Invaluable in testing and providing feedback, these feet are called gold standards by their companies. The data sheets of these models, which record their measurements from calf and shin (to account for boots) through the arch and instep

---

18. Benzecry, *The Perfect Fit*. Thanks to Vicky Hattam for sharing this reference.

to the length of the toes, provide evidence of the inevitable irregularity of feet. Right and left feet are not always symmetrical in one person, never mind the swathes of potential consumers who must also find a fit. Yet it is the fit model who makes the standardized shoe possible. A live foot, mobile, distinctive and malleable, can convey way more information to the designer and technician than a standardized and stiff shoe last. Working with the same model over time allows the designers, technicians, and production managers for a brand to "stabilize" the foot, to understand measurements, the stage of production, the difference between drawings, prototypes, and samples. They learn to work with the irregularities and idiosyncrasies of the model's legs and feet, such as low calves, pronation, or a high instep.

Shoes are manufactured to calibrate to a U.S. standard size, 6B or 7B, the reasons for which are obscured in fuzzy speculations about once common sizes, but a model does more than conform to a measurement. It may take a few seasons for a model to become more than a foot and it takes at least a year to give useful feedback. She must manage her weight, exercise, shape or anything that might change the information her foot provides when she steps onto the table. An experienced foot model acquires a modicum of technical knowledge and can provide solutions. Fit models give the final go-ahead that confirms that a shoe is what it should be to meet the specifications for large orders. It takes a few rounds of fitting and discussion between the model and the team before a last is produced for the assembly line. Unbeknownst to its owner, every toe about to take the plunge in new footwear will walk in the footprints of another.

The standardization of sizes has its roots in the nineteenth century, when the measurement of bodies was being undertaken for statistical and anthropometric purposes. The quirks or singularities of individuals or the documentation of variation would eventually become deviations from standards or folded into racialized scientific investigations. Belgian astronomer Alphonse Quetelet came up with the statistical concept of the "average man" in the 1830s. A few decades later, French policeman Alphonse Bertillon produced an early system of biometric identification, which consisted of eleven precise measurements of the body, from the length and breadth of the head to the width of the cheek to the forearm and foot to the right ear. He added to this the photograph, which is where his legacy remains—in the police mugshot—and at the urging of statistician and eugenicist, Francis Galton, he also included fingerprints, although he did not have much faith in them. The most significant identificatory marker before the advent of DNA testing, fingerprinting was ultimately fully developed in India, where the colonial government, engaged in cartographic triangulation, was keen on a comparable imaging of its people, flora, and fauna, which classification was aided by scientists and anthropologists.[19]

Fit, the idea that dress or footwear can hug protectively yet be fluid, is paradoxically a result of a long process of producing bodies and self-conceptions whose fitness has been under scrutiny. In the 1960s, two doctors in Jaipur, India, noticed a cobbler unable to hunker down as he needed to in order to do his work because of his rigid prosthetic limb. The prosthesis generally available at the time was the Solid Ankle Cushioned Foot (SACH), developed in the United States in the 1940s and '50s, which consisted of a stable foot with a firm heel and no lateral movement or articulation of the ankle. The SACH was relatively light and durable,

---

19. Sengoopta, Chandak, *Imprint of the Raj*.

and offered amputees the possibility of wearing different kinds of shoes. However, for people who tended to squat, go barefoot, or sit on the ground, it was inflexible and cumbersome.

No prosthetic is a one-size-fits-all. It must be adapted to fit the owner. Even when it simulates the other limb, people must relearn how to walk to achieve their customary gait. The residual limb has its own sensations and a fitting process can take months to mold the stump, shape it with a shrink sock, create a cast for a prosthetic limb on which the person must learn to bear weight. If it doesn't fit, the skin might break down, resulting in infections that make walking difficult. P.K. Sethi, one of the two Indian doctors, was professor of orthopedic surgery at a hospital. Together with his colleague and former professor in the School of Arts and Crafts, Ramchandra Sharma, who was working with disabled people at the hospital, he took on the challenge of finding a solution for amputees with bodily practices that differed completely from those assumed by the SACH.[20]

A human foot at its ankle is capable of both plantar flexion (imagine pointing your toes) and dorsiflexion (bring the toes back and point them toward your shin). Dorsiflexion is essential for someone who wants to squat or sit on the floor. Many craftspeople contributed to the research of Sethi, Sharma, and others—cobblers, metal workers, carpenters, tire retreaders—to arrive at the final design of what has come to be known as the Jaipur Foot. The foot of this prosthesis was divided into three separate blocks, the hind foot, the ankle, and the forefoot, made from rubber and wood. The calf was shaped with aluminum, waterproofed, covered with vulcanized rubber, and painted in the appropriate skin tone. A slot between the

---

20. The account of the Jaipur Foot is based on the following: Arya and Klenerman, "The Jaipur Foot"; Rao, "A Firm Footing for the Disabled"; Srinivasan, "Technology Sits Cross-Legged."

big toe and the next allowed sandals to be worn. The flexibility this offered allowed the user to sit on the floor, work in the fields, climb trees, squat, sit cross-legged, and, because of its appearance, which did not presume a shoe, go barefoot.

Handcrafted using ordinary, easily available materials, the Jaipur Foot was inexpensive. Material equivalents could be locally sourced in other countries and local artisans familiar with their usage could be trained to manufacture limbs. Nonliterate artisans can visually gauge a person's requirements and fit a foot in a relatively short period of time—observers describe feet being fitted in as little as an hour, with seven days for a fitting below the knees, and longer for one above the knee. Dr. Sethi did not take out a patent on the foot, allowing it to be adapted to local contexts, materials, and skills, but this lack of standardization has meant that the quality of production and fitting is not assured. The Jaipur Foot has been widely used in low-income contexts and in countries such as Afghanistan, Angola, Cambodia, Tanzania, and Vietnam, which are dealing with landmine injuries and other aftereffects of war.

Medical prostheses are a less noticed part of the industrial infrastructure concomitant with war. During the American Civil War, there were about sixty thousand amputations of various limbs; in fact, three-fourths of operations were amputations, sometimes done to avoid gangrene.[21] After the war, the federal government provided artificial limbs and government pensions for documented Union soldiers who had suffered amputations. Considered rebels, Confederate soldiers were not entitled to limbs or federal compensation, and it was left to the southern states to bear the cost and set up their own programs. The prosthetic limb

---

21. Figg and Farrell-Beck, "Amputation in the Civil War."

Union veteran of the Civil War with his prostheses. Albumen print on card, 1890. Photograph: W. E. Bowman. Courtesy: Library of Congress.

industry boomed at this time, with an enormous number of applications for patents, especially for lower limb assistive technologies such as legs, crutches, and wheelchairs, even though more men survived with upper limb amputations. It became normal to see men on crutches with pinned up sleeves and trouser legs, symbolizing bravery and service to the nation.

It was only shortly before the war that the word "normal" had come to mean adhering to or conforming to a rule, something usual or regular. Disability scholar Lennard Davis draws attention to the fact that the meaning of norm as standard or an average entered usage between 1840 and 1860.[22] Prior to this, a carpenter's square had been called a "norm" and the word generally meant perpendicular or standing at right angles. This geometric formulation extended its meaning to encompass other social, cultural, and bodily aspects of human life just when the proliferation of artificial limbs was unsettling what it means to be upright.

How tempting it is to think that all one needs to walk is a good fit. The foot has been evacuated from the shoe for a while now by the systems of control that obscure the circumstances of their creation. Obscured is the policing, the molding, the transformation of journeys into lines, the demand for exactitude, the ignoring of the bony protuberance, the splayed toes, the callus, the creation of a world in which footwear is civilized and required, in which the footprint is inevitably a shoeprint into which a foot is made to fit. The footprint of a bare foot is often sentimental, like that of a newborn at a hospital or the pawprint of a beloved dog. Looking for the print of the now-absent foot reminds us of who is immobilized by regimes of fit. But might it also suggest that we can walk *in* but without fitting *into* the footprints of others? Not to strut our singularity but to walk with an insistence on the abundant, rich, and plentiful variety of human bodies and the ways in which they inhabit this much more than human world.

22. Davis, "Introduction: Normality, Power and Culture."

ITINERARY 3

TRUDGE

Pounding the Pavement

In 1986, British-Palestinian artist Mona Hatoum inked footprints onto the streets of Sheffield, in Northern England, stamped with the word "Unemployed." Although a steel-producing powerhouse since the nineteenth century, by the late 1970s Sheffield had begun to see the unmistakable effects of the post-war decline in the demand for steel. In 1980, steelworkers had been part of the national British Steel strike, a harbinger of industrial disputes to come, most significantly the 1984–85 miners' strike, which also started in Yorkshire. The economic situation exposed by these industrial actions was dire. Hatoum's intervention underscored one of the effects of this collapse. A photograph of the artist shows her crouched on the pavement, dressed in black, the words "Artist at Work" in white on her back, using a linocut stencil in the shape of the sole of a shoe to leave the imprints.[1]

In 2018, this piece was featured in a group exhibition called

---

1. White Cube, "Mona Hatoum at the Millennium Gallery, Sheffield."

Hope Is Strong at the Millennium Gallery in Sheffield. No longer presented as a performance, it appeared now as a paired set of images—one showing the artist stenciling the footprints on the sidewalk, the other a document showing a stencil sole accompanied by the text of the original proposal she had made for the performance. Hatoum proposed walking the streets with an inking pad and roller and, with every step she took, she would ink the word "Unemployed" from the bottom of her shoe, only stopping when a footprint had been created for every single unemployed person in Sheffield.

Only one year before Hatoum made her Sheffield shoeprints, in May 1985, had she taken her bare feet for a walk in another political performance in London. Called "Roadworks," part of an exhibition of the same name in Brixton, this is the better-known of her early performance works.[2] Brixton was an Afro-Caribbean working-class neighborhood in London facing the effects of recession and civic neglect, with poor housing, high crime, rampant unemployment, and racial tensions. In 1981, there had been a series of violent confrontations prompted by racist policing, especially the excessive use of stop-and-search in the area. In an hour-long performance, Hatoum left the gallery to walk in unshod feet with a pair of Doc Martens tied by their laces to her ankles.

Video documentation of the piece shows the tiled pavement with patches of damp. Cars go by, as does an occasional baby carriage, and so do men's and women's feet in a variety of shoes. And there is Hatoum, her black coveralls rolled up above her ankles, bare feet laced to boots that follow behind. The boots were as

---

2. Archer et al., *Mona Hatoum*.

much a symbol of the police as of skinheads and punks. To keep them upright the artist had to walk slowly, giving the relatively light Doc Martens the added appearance of a burden. Several people stand looking perplexed, staring at her feet. Hatoum, who wanted to take her work to a non-art audience, says she enjoyed the passing observations of this ad hoc public. "Do you know you're being followed?" asked one man. "What's going on?" asked another, to which a Black woman answered, "She's being followed by the police."[3] Ten years later, Hatoum extracted a still from the video, cropped and printed it as a black and white photograph before mounting it on aluminum. "Performance Still 1985/1995," always displayed on the floor leaning against the wall, shows only the lower legs in motion, bare feet with the boots attached, on a tiled pavement. The residue of damp weather is evident in the wet partial print of someone's shoe sole beside the foot of her bent left leg. The angle of the forward left knee and the limp left hand convey work and weariness. Brixton has fallen away in this photograph, leaving only the incongruity of bare feet on a city street.[4]

Urban design is ambivalent about feet. Asphalt, Walter Benjamin notes in his Konvolut M on the flâneur, was first used for pavements.[5] Although uninviting to a bare foot, the even layering of asphalt or concrete on the sidewalks that arose beside streets in the mid-nineteenth century city made flânerie or indeed any city walking easier, just as macadam and tar made streets smoother for cars and carriages. Vehicular traffic moved faster, and so could the

3. Perrot, "Mona Hatoum, Performance Still 1985–95."
4. Archer et al., op. cit.
5. Benjamin, *The Arcades Project*, 427.

Mona Hatoum, "Performance Still 1985/1995." Black and white photograph mounted on aluminum, 30 1/8 x 42 1/2 in. (76.5 x 108 cm) © Mona Hatoum. Photo © Stephen White. Courtesy White Cube.

pedestrians beside them accelerate, even as both surfaces resisted the imprint of their users. The footfalls of the avowedly anonymous urban crowd were unregistered. In any case, as a largely paved carapace became emblematic of the metropolis, urbanity itself became synonymous with shod feet. Only an artist at work might still visibly trace the impact on these surfaces of those pounding the pavement in search of jobs. And yet at times, if only briefly, a few pawprints, birds' feet, the squish and oops of a shoeprint in the freshly poured concrete of a sidewalk, mark the tracks of urban inhabitants, just as a tree root makes its underground presence known by flexing a limb past paved surfaces.

Street trees had been the focus of almost a decade's worth of protest in Sheffield when the *Hope Is Strong* exhibition opened in 2018. The city council had determined that they would remove trees whose roots had cracked pavements and curbs or made them uneven in order to make necessary upgrades to roads, pavements, and street lights. Over five thousand trees were slated for removal. This proposed mass felling of largely healthy trees provoked massive protests, which turned violent at times with arrests and threats of legal action. The council had intended to plant saplings after repairs but these would in no way match the shade and beauty of mature trees. The council had also assumed that evening out pavements and filling in potholes would be an evident urban priority—and so it was for many but not at the expense of trees. According to a report in *The Guardian*, in 2019 a team of experts was brought in to look at a random selection of trees to see if repairs could be made to the pavement without felling them.[6] In one case, the inspectors dug into the asphalt to see what damage the

---

6. Shackle, "Chainsaws, Disguises and Toxic Tea."

tree's roots had done only to discover that its roots were nowhere near the surface. In this and several other instances, the culprit was the asphalt, repeatedly laid over where roots had slightly lifted the pavement, ultimately resulting in an uneven surface. Most trees were no threat to the city's paved ground cover.

Edifice/Embodiment

In April 2003, the Lower Manhattan Development Corporation (LMDC) in New York announced a competition for a memorial for the World Trade Center site to remember those who had been killed in the attacks of September 11, 2001.[7] Applicants were asked to demonstrate five physical program elements in their submissions. Two were straightforward: to recognize each individual victim and to provide an area for quiet contemplation. Two of them, more unusually, asked for a place for family members and loved ones as well as a separate accessible resting place for unidentified remains. The fifth was distinctive: to make visible the footprints of the original World Trade Center towers. The design that won the competition, by Michael Arad, delivered on this, placing two voids with flowing water in the footprints of the towers. Landscape architect Peter Walker added rows of swamp oak trees. As the voids stood for absence and grief, the trees signaled rebirth and resilience. Many commentators have asked however why response to catastrophic loss zeroed in on the footprints of the towers. And indeed, we might add, when did buildings begin to leave footprints?

It is to 1969 that the *Oxford English Dictionary* (OED) dates the earliest reference to the footprint's meaning as the surface area

---

7. LMDC, "World Trade Center Site Memorial Competition Guidelines."

occupied by a structure or device—as it happens, not long after construction had begun in 1968 for the original World Trade Center.[8] This was an extension from the footprint's meaning as the landing area for spacecraft that William Safire had remarked upon in his etymology of the term, which had come into usage only earlier that decade. The footprint in its most direct meaning—the imprint of a foot or shoe—entered the English language in the sixteenth century and had not wandered much more beyond that, generally signifying a trace all the way to the early twentieth century. At that point, it inched further to incorporate the impression of vehicle tires which, after all, do carry the weight of moving bodies. However, between the time of the Twin Towers' inauguration in 1973 and their demise in 2001, the footprint had begun to signify the solidity of buildings as unmistakably as it once did the agility of feet.

In 2002, the Governor of New York, George Pataki, in the middle of a re-election campaign, swore that the World Trade Center footprints would always be "a lasting memorial for those who were lost," thereby mandating the resulting rebuilding response.[9] When Daniel Libeskind, the architect first hired to create the master plan for the site, made a presentation of his proposal, titled "Memory Foundations," there it was in white on black: an outline of the site depicting the two squares of the twin buildings with two firm lines leading out from them to the label "Footprints." Absence guided the primary narrative at Ground Zero, says Marita Sturken, and trying to resolve it is what produced the fixation with the buildings, and in addition the aesthetic emphasis on the void as a response.[10]

8. *Oxford English Dictionary* (OED), n.d. Accessed June 9, 2022.
9. Wyatt, "Pataki's Surprising Limit on Ground Zero Design."
10. Sturken, "Containing Absence, Shaping Presence at Ground Zero."

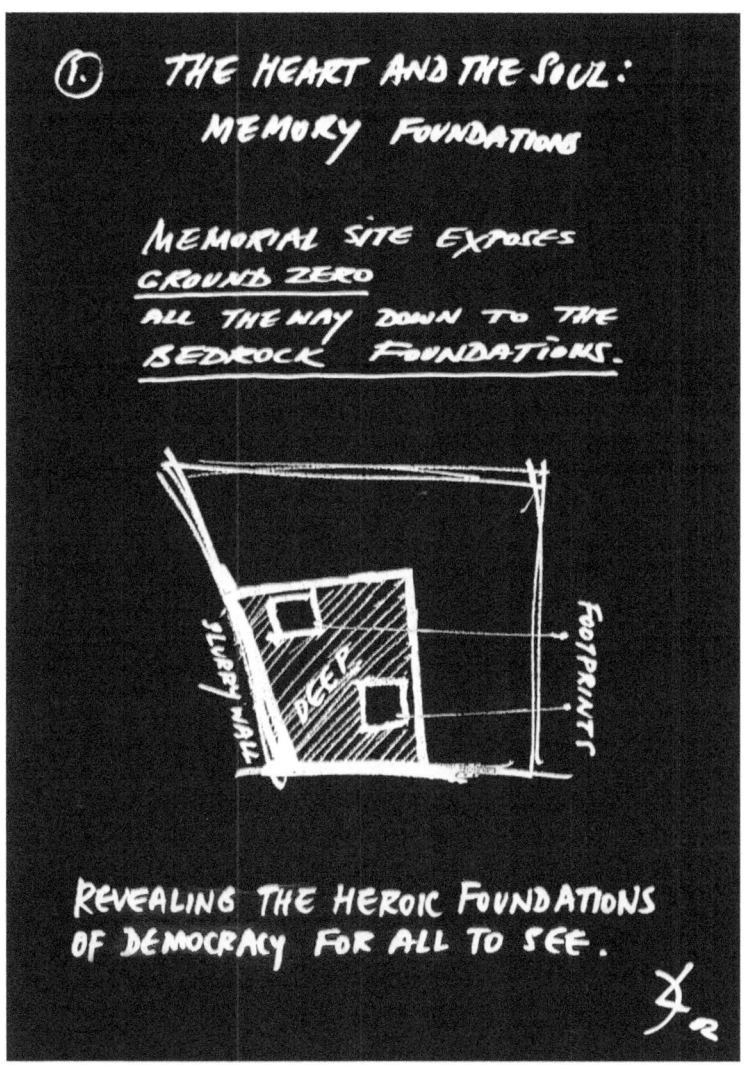

From Daniel Libeskind's proposal to the Lower Manhattan Development Corporation. Credit: Daniel Libeskind. Courtesy of Libeskind Studio.

It was not from a void however that the original World Trade Center itself had arisen. Until the 1940s, the area had been home to Syrian immigrants who had established a vibrant community with shops, churches, and restaurants, dating to the late nineteenth century.[11] Robert Moses, New York's larger than life urban planning czar, who rewrote the face of the city's urban fabric by municipal fiat, was the first to strike through this. He acquired the area by eminent domain and razed it to build the Brooklyn Battery Tunnel. In the 1950s, a concerted effort grew among key business and political leaders, primarily negotiated by David Rockefeller, Chair of Chase Manhattan Bank, with the support of his brother, Nelson Rockefeller, the governor of New York State, to spur development in the area.[12] There was a lively commercial strip of small radio, television, and electronic shops, but they wanted something with a big footprint, akin to Rockefeller Center uptown. Radio Row was demolished, with the expectation that the new office complex would bring Lower Manhattan out of an economic slump. The soaring office towers and grand open plazas of the resulting World Trade Center were not particularly beloved of the city—and they, in turn, were completely unsympathetic to the daily interactions and rhythms of city life—although the transit hub below, with its many shops, was in active use in their lifetime.

Nevertheless, once buildings themselves had become embodied, it is no surprise that the magnitude of human loss after 9/11 found just expression in the image of two towers whose unmistakable contours had long defined the city's skyline. Urban footprints have nothing to do with human feet but so well entrenched

11. Schulz, "The History of Little Syria."
12. Goldberger, *Up from Zero*

had they become in architecture and urban planning vocabulary that they served as a strange outsize double for people. Architects played no small role in their exaltation on the site, according to Philip Nobel.[13] The formal cue that the trace of the buildings provided was the sort of direction relished by architects when faced with an empty site: the footprints were basically a crutch.

Early on, in the immediate aftermath of September 11, others characterized the destroyed buildings as missing limbs. Artists Paul Myoda and Julian LaVerdiere had been working on a public art project of bioluminescent beacons that was to be installed atop the World Trade Center. When they looked at the ghostly site, harshly lit by searchlights, they felt they could almost see and feel the absent buildings—as if they were phantom limbs that ache even when they are no longer there.[14] Just weeks after 9/11, they created a visual rendering of two beams in the shape of the towers rising into the skyline for the *New York Times Magazine*, which described the image as "refilling the void left by the twin towers with incandescence."[15] Six months later, this became a reality on the site in the form of a physical installation of twin beams called "Tribute in Light." The artists had intended it as a symbolic but temporary installation; however, it proved so popular that it has become a feature of the annual 9/11 commemoration ever since. According to the 9/11 Memorial and Museum, which now oversees the tribute, these dual beams of eighty-eight xenon bulbs of 7,000-watts each reach 4 miles into the sky and can be viewed from a 60-mile radius around Lower Manhattan.[16]

---

13. Nobel, *Sixteen Acres*, 253.
14. Heim, "Co-Creator of Tribute of Light at Ground Zero Reflects."
15. *New York Times*, "Filling the Void."
16. 9/11 Memorial and Museum, "Tribute in Light,"

These limbs cross the path of other journeys. Several species of birds make their migratory voyages, flying across New York at night at the same time of year as the commemoration. Attracted to the insects who are themselves attracted to the light, birds and bats get caught in its beam, becoming confused, circling, calling, unable to find their way out. The power of the lights disorients and exhausts birds, who then frequently collide with the glass windows of buildings near the site.[17] NYC Bird Alliance (formerly NYC Audubon), scientists, and volunteers have been gathering for many years to monitor the situation. When the number of birds trapped in the beams reaches about a thousand, the lights are switched off for twenty minutes. In a given evening, the lights may be switched off seven or eight times.[18] This inadequate solution allows birds to disperse and go on their way so that the city can stretch its wounded limb and imprint its phantom footprint on the skies.

Boots on the Ground/Shoes in the Air

Twenty years after 9/11, the United States was trying to disentangle itself from Afghanistan, where it had been mired in conflict ever since. Immediately after the attacks, the U.S., in October 2001, had invaded Afghanistan, to track down Osama bin Laden, and because the Taliban was believed to have supported the perpetrators. In 2003, once this had expanded to a war on terror in general, the U.S. invaded Iraq, claiming that the country had "weapons of mass destruction" and that its leader, Saddam Hussein, was aiding and abetting Al-Qaeda. These wars proved relentless and

---

17. Van Doren et al., "High-Intensity Urban Light Installation."

18. Barnard, "The 9/11 Tribute Lights Are Endangering 160,000 Birds a Year."

costly in every sense. President Obama took office promising to withdraw "boots on the ground," a phrase that became ubiquitous political usage at the time.[19]

A large-scale combat operation had not been the U.S. intention for these invasions. The Secretary of Defense under President Bush, Donald Rumsfeld, was keen to deploy his new approach to military operations. He wanted future forces to be mobile, capable of acting across distances, striking swiftly and precisely with devastating effects. This required greater reliance on technology, intelligence, and air power. The shadow of the U.S. experience in Vietnam hung over all military strategy, as did more recent peacekeeping and humanitarian missions in the Balkans and Somalia. The Army was reluctant to abandon conventional warfare but there was a general feeling in the Bush administration that sending thousands of troops to other countries to deal with their problems—even if these were caused by the U.S. or relevant to U.S. interests in the region—was an expensive and ineffective strategy. Military historian David Fitzgerald says that Rumsfeld's fondness for an extremely light footprint and limited involvement in postwar reconstructive efforts greatly influenced the Iraq offensive.[20]

The Bush administration misled the country about the so-called weapons of mass destruction; they wanted to topple Saddam Hussein and try out what the media was to call the Rumsfeld Doctrine. "Shock and Awe" was a military strategy that had been introduced in the 1990s: the enemy would be sapped of the will to fight by an immense show of power. This underlay the plan for Iraq. But the enemy in the Global War on Terrorism inherently has different attributes from a conventional opponent. The air

---

19. Traub, "The Empty Threat of 'Boots on the Ground.'"
20. Fitzgerald, "Mr. Rumsfeld's War."

force and navy might bomb or shell targets but the army had to be on the ground and they frequently faced counter-insurgencies. Critics have pointed out that "shock and awe" is all very good for the immediate disabling of enemy power but it runs the risk of destroying systems and infrastructure, making it necessary to take responsibility for basic governance. Rumsfeld's footprint had no plan for civilian handover.

The light footprint strategy became the U.S.'s preferred approach from the Bush into the Obama years. Relying on technology with boots off the ground was seen as a better sell to a public removed from the immediacy of 9/11, weary of the war and also critical of the U.S.'s response to terror. Major Fernando M. Lujan, writing for the Center for New American Security, a Washington D.C. think tank focused on national security issues, says that the light footprint is responsive to budgetary issues, continual deployment, and security challenges.[21] However, a surgical strike or "shock and awe" can only be one aspect of a strategy; he says it has to be followed up with a plan for phasing out the military and coordinating with civilian leadership, and engaging pre-emptively with local groups—requiring other training, like cultural knowledge, negotiating techniques, and language skills.

The legacy of a footprint is surely measured by its effect rather than its intention. No matter how hard you stamp on dry sand, it leaves little impression. Conversely, a light footprint can have a heavy effect—ask those in Afghanistan or Iraq. In 2008, President George W. Bush and Iraqi Prime Minister Nouri al-Maliki held a joint press conference to announce a new U.S.-Iraq security agreement, which included a plan for U.S. troop withdrawal.

---

21. Lujan, "Light Footprints."

Iraqi journalist Muntadhar al-Zaidi was in the audience. He had his own plan and was prepared—he recorded his will, handed his ring and wallet to his colleagues. He was also wearing slip-on footwear.[22] When Bush reiterated that the war was not over, al-Zaidi took off his shoe and threw it at him, shouting, "This is a farewell kiss from the Iraqi people, dog." Bush dodged it. Al-Zaidi threw the second shoe, shouting, "This is from widows, orphans, and those who were killed in Iraq."[23] The prime minister intercepted that shoe. Al-Zaidi was wrestled to the ground, beaten, and given a three-year prison sentence.

The following year, in 2009, a giant fiberglass and copper shoe was installed in Tikrit, Saddam Hussein's hometown. This was taken down the following day by government officials.[24] Western commentators have repeatedly emphasized the cultural meaning of the shoe as an insult in Arab culture, but even without much cultural knowhow, most understood the impetus behind the shoe sufficiently for it to circulate widely on social media. The foot's symbolic power is in its duality, simultaneously abject and defiant. The meaning of its footprint is relational. Its impact—light or heavy—is not determined by its owner; that prerogative rests with those on whom it lands.

Cement Shoes

In April 2016, nine women sat in a row with their feet encased in cement in front of the presidential palace in Jakarta, Indonesia. As sore as they surely were, having walked over three hundred miles from their village in the Kendeng Mountains of Central Java to the capital city, they placed their feet in wooden boxes and had

22. Heller, "An Oral History of the George W. Bush Shoe Throwing."
23. Ramadani, "The Shoes We Longed For."
24. Sturcke, "Soleful Tribute."

Kartini Kendeng cement protest, Jakarta, 2017. Credit: Stephanie Tangkilisan. Courtesy of the photographer.

cement poured over them. The cement weighed about 15 pounds on each foot so the women were effectively immovable, anchored in place. Wet cement burns bare skin. To avoid chemical burn, a plaster cast covered each foot, except for the toes. Through slits in the boxes the women could thrust their toes out and expose them. This was crucial for medical oversight, to ensure that the feet were not permanently damaged.[25]

They had been protesting for several years against the destructive environmental impact of a cement factory in their region. The women were popularly referred to as "Kartini Kendeng," a name

---

25. This account of the cement protests is drawn from the following: Barahamin, "Kendeng against Cement."; Firdaus, "The Women of Kendeng."; Lie and Tangkilisan, "Episode 26: Kartini Kendeng"; Watchdoc Documentary, "SAMIN vs SEMEN."

derived from Indonesia's icon of women's empowerment, Raden Adjeng Kartini. A key progressive figure of the colonial period, Kartini was a noblewoman by birth, from the same part of the country as these women. Kartini spent her relatively brief life (she died at age 25) using her position to improve women's lives, particularly by supporting education. Her birthday is celebrated annually as Kartini Day. The women with cement feet were seen as following in her footsteps and aware of it.

The landscape of the Kendeng Mountains, which stretches over a hundred miles across several regencies, is karst. Karst is formed when water interacts with soluble rocks, like limestone, dolomite, and gypsum, dissolving its way through sedimentary layers to create subterranean networks of caves, rivers, and springs. This distinctive ecosystem sustains the flooded fields required for rice-paddy cultivation and also supports drier fields of maize and soybean. It also nurtures an enormous variety of plant and animal life. It is the limestone that the cement industry covets. Quarries and mines would deplete the groundwater upon which the livelihood of people and the life of the area depended. The women had wrapped their feet in gypsum plaster, a mineral integral to the topography of their mountains, to protect them against the cement that they sensed would ravage their life-worlds.

The mountains are home to a singular community, called the Sedulur Sikep or Samin, who follow the teachings of a nineteenth century leader, Samin Surosentiko. "Sedulur" means sibling and "Sikep" refers to those who embrace or are alert and responsible. Samin's movement was anti-colonial, fuelled by the displacement of people from forest lands, but it was also spiritual and social. His followers refused to pay the taxes levied by the Dutch colonial government and withdrew from its corvée labor regimes. They embraced his precepts, eschewing trade or government employment and refusing formal schooling. Instead, they live as agriculturists, rejecting the notion of land as property that can be bought and sold, fostering a spiritual respect for the land and all it offers. They are a largely self-reliant community who retain the distance from the state that is central to their origin, frequently refusing to fill in the blank for religious affiliation on the state identity card. Cement mining threatened a way of life integrated into ecological rhythms but resistance to it also tapped into a long vein of civil disobedience among the Sedulur Sikep. They have been at the forefront of the agitation although the movement has grown to include affected communities who espouse other beliefs, across the Kendeng region.

The struggle in the Kendeng Mountains has been going on since 2006, when the first cement factory was proposed by PT Semen Gresik, later PT Semen, a publicly traded state-owned enterprise. Samin communities rose up in opposition, even filing a case in court. In 2009, they won the case—a plan that had been put in place in a protected area with no community consultation was rejected. But this was no more than a delay for the cement industry. Environmental protections for part of the area were overturned in 2010, opening the door once more for industry and mining. In 2012, PT Indocement, a subsidiary of the Heidelberg Cement Group, started its environmental impact survey, with a view to moving in. At the same time, PT Semen, which had lost the case, simply moved from one regency to another. Agitation continued. The cement industry had the support of district government, which overlooked environmental protections in favor of industrial growth. The villagers with the support of NGOs filed another suit in 2015, which was thrown out on technical grounds.

In 2016, PT Semen Indonesia started the construction of their factory. By the time they resorted to cementing their feet in the capital, the Kartini Kendeng and many others had been resisting the cement industry for years, demonstrating outside the factory, setting up tent encampments, facing arrest and intimidation.

In August 2016, Indonesia's then-president Joko Widodo met the women and promised to halt operations and reopen the environmental assessment study. In October, the Supreme Court upheld the lawsuit the Samin had brought, citing environmental concerns. The company's permit was revoked. In an attempt to sidestep this ruling, the governor of Central Java issued an addendum that offered a loophole for new licenses. When this was met with outrage, he was forced to revoke the addendum, only to issue a new environmental permit in February 2017 to PT Semen, giving them the green light to continue. The women were back in Jakarta in March that year, with their feet encased in cement once more. The protest was larger this time, with about ten additional people joining each day, until over fifty people sat with cemented feet. "Cement shoes" is an expression associated with criminal groups like the Mafia and refers to the murder or disposal of a victim in water while weighed down with concrete, to ensure that the body will not surface. In 2017, the cement shoes of the protesters had such a deadly effect: one of the women died. The president met one of the grief-stricken protesters once more, but he offered no definite assurances, lobbing the responsibility back to the governor. The struggle continues.

Indonesia is one of the world's leading producers of cement, an industry with a large carbon footprint. Traditional cement production contributes to high carbon emissions, air pollution, and the diminishment of the water table. In 2022–2023, the Kendeng region faced extensive flooding, which environmentalists and activists believe is caused by the effects of deforestation, mining, and the loss of environmental protections. The destruction of vegetation by mines and quarries loosens soil and thereby the capacity to hold water.[26] Ironically, overcapacity confronts the industry—much more cement is produced than utilized. In 2023, the government acknowledged that this was particularly the case in Java.[27]

In August 2024, Indonesia celebrated the 79th year of independence in the proposed new capital of Nusantara, on the island of Borneo.[28] The city was nowhere near ready for the celebrations, but construction continued apace. Indonesia's historic capital, Jakarta, is sinking. This is due to a fatal confluence of factors—uncontrolled groundwater extraction to support a dense, growing population and the rising sea levels of worldwide climate change. The solution to this has been to transplant the capital to the jungles of East Kalimantan, in Borneo, whose trees can be razed to render a clean slate, and where new infrastructure projects promise employment and the need for more cement.

The contradictions of cement—integral to our built environment, inimical to the natural world—are not unique to Indonesia. Yet, the protest movement in Kendeng, in opposing cement to karst, brings into view the transfer of power from one conception of the footprint to another. Cement exudes strength, certainty, the implacable weight of presence. Karst presumes reliance on an unseen world of caves, sinkholes, and underground waterways. Asphalt once promised ease of circulation, the onrush of an im-

26. Candraningrum, "Forget Kendeng Not."
27. CemNet.com: "Indonesia Remains Gripped by Cement Overcapacity."
28. Llewellyn, "Nusantara."

mense, lithe, and heterogeneous urban crowd that buoyed new arrivals and enthralled urban commentators. Creativity, culture, and movement were sustained by this built world, making possible both the bright lights of ambition and the autonomy of multiple shadows. When rampant urban construction seems to cater only to the few, the corpulent complacency of building footprints mocks the ordinary walker. Anyone who has mistakenly stepped on a freshly laid sidewalk will tell you that a foot pressed into cement is not easily relinquished. But where the sole meets tender ground, it is much more likely to find a foothold again in the future.

Brick Feet

In 2016, when the women were cementing their feet in Indonesia, the Indian artist Birender Yadav created a work called *Walking on the Roof of Hell*.[29] It consisted of a set of *khadau*s, makeshift wooden sandals with a couple of ropes as thongs or a piece of fabric as a strap. When he installs the work, the khadaus are arranged in an artful circle or else placed casually as if their owners had just slipped them off. Accompanying the footwear is a set of photographs of the feet of these owners, bare, splayed flat, and cracked, in the khadaus. The khadaus in turn are blackened, sweat-stained, bearing the marks of the feet that once inhabited them. They belong to workers at a brick factory in Mirzapur, in the state of Uttar Pradesh in Northern India, who work the kilns where bricks are fired to strengthen them. In the absence of any protective gear,

---

29. This account is based on an interview with the artist on May 20, 2022, and on materials he shared thereafter.

they fashion khadaus to shield their feet against the searing temperatures of the kilns, atop which they work. Often, they must wrap their feet in cloth before they insert them into the khadau, to protect them against the unbearable heat.

Yadav had been working with the brick kiln workers in Mirzapur for several years when he made this piece. His attention had been drawn to their feet from the start. Most of the brick-workers are migrants, often from tribal communities in other states, who walk considerable distances to get to this seasonal employment, which is terminated with the monsoon. For the rest of the year, they must find other jobs, which are rarely assured. This precariousness propels them to take advances from the agents, who recruit brick-workers each season, frequently pushing them into conditions of debt bondage. Many brick-worker families have been doing this work for generations. Working atop the brick kiln to produce bricks of different qualities requires particular skill, the knowledge often passed down in families, but its duration is finite. These specialized workers don't last more than five years before they succumb to foot injuries and loss of sensation. Yadav made an early work called "Common Foot Problems," akin to a reflexology chart or poster in a doctor's office. It showed the soles of the feet with arrows pointing to conditions, such as "Bruised," "Exhausted," "Fatigued," "Without Food," "Cut," "Scabbed," "Disappointed." It was blunt.

The core of Yadav's multidisciplinary practice, however, has been rooted in an ongoing relationship with the workers and their families. While they are working in the brick factory, the workers live in homes made out of unfired bricks, homes that are destroyed when they leave. Children accompany them but are also left behind in the care of an older child or another worker as a

Birender Yadav. Detail of feet wearing khadaus, from *Walking on the Roof of Hell*, 2016, archival print. © Birender Yadav. Courtesy of the artist.

mother must move elsewhere for work. Some children are put to work themselves. Yadav began to do art workshops with the young children. His files are filled with photographs of them, knees and feet covered in brick dust, hands smudged with clay, intent on their craft. They pose their sinuous and layered clay sculptures for a photograph in front of the stacks of rectangular bricks that their parents carry from the kilns. Women balance several bricks on their head while men heft a carrying pole on their shoulder with two loads of bricks. They are given a token for each load that they must collect and store carefully for a week so that they get paid.

Donkeys and horses also carry bricks to and fro. Pairs of animals, often yoked to one another, carry panniers loaded with bricks on either side. Donkeys, mules, and horses are a widespread feature of South Asia's brick kilns. They may be acquired seasonally for the brick factory as a source of income for their owners. They are often transported in cramped conditions and treated poorly. The brick workers identify with the animals, whose conditions mirror their own. Yadav's 2015 piece, *Donkey Worker*, was prompted by hearing several workers refer to themselves as *gadha*s or donkeys. It was the image of a donkey made entirely out of their purple inked thumbprints. The *angootha chhap* or thumbprint is the widespread equivalent of a signature, the identity mark of an unlettered population. The same year, he created another work, *Erased Faces*, in which he asked the workers to place their thumbprints across the portrait of their own faces, taken as they might be for an identity document.

The way in which the body of the worker collides with the identificatory demands of state bureaucracies and of employers has preoccupied Yadav since he was a student. These bodies bear the lasting imprints of back-breaking work—fissured and deadened feet, shoulders permanently grooved with the mark of the carrying pole—and yet recognition eludes these workers. When he was doing his master's degree in Delhi, he overheard some laborers speaking Khortha in the construction sites of the new metro system. The language is from the state of Jharkhand (formerly part of Bihar) in eastern India where Yadav had himself grown up, in the coal mining city of Dhanbad. He started talking to the workers, getting to know them, taking photographs, idly considering some sort of art project. Suspicious though they were at first, taking him to be a government employee, the workers were soon enlisting his help to deal with government bureaucracies.

India's new universal identity system, the Aadhar, was being introduced at the time. This is a twelve-digit identity number given to residents of India on the basis of biometric and domiciliary information. Originally and officially intended to be voluntary, to provide streamlined and easier access to public services such as unemployment, food and fuel rations, or medical care, the system has now overtaken every aspect of daily life and is demanded willy-nilly at every point of formal transaction, even those unrelated to the government. The metro workers wanted an Aadhar to get paid. However, their hands were so badly calloused and worn that they could rarely provide the requisite fingerprints for biometrics. In addition, like the brick kiln workers, many of them were migrants and unable to offer the proof of a stable address that is also required by the Aadhar.

Yadav began to understand that his photographs and videos were not material for a stand-alone project but part of a documentary research process inextricably tied to sustained relationships. It was over cups of tea with the metro workers and during breaks with those in the kilns that he began to collect thumbprints for his two works. In his artwork, he began to insist on the presence of the workers through their traces—the inked residue of their thumbs, the footprint of the worker soaked into the khadau by sweat and smoke. For his 2016 installation, he had had to trade with the owners to collect the thirty pairs of khadaus he needed. He offered to make them new ones with better rope but they gravitated to the familiarity of their own footwear. In any case, they said, they would not wear it for long. Their feet would eventually turn into brick.

War Un-memorial

Across from the Latin Bridge beneath which the Miljacka River flows brown and muddy are the duck-footed footprints. Mortar shells assailed the city from the surrounding hills when it withstood one of the longest sieges in modern history. The footprints disappeared.[30] Other marks appeared on streets and sidewalks across the city where artillery shells fell gouging the asphalt and concrete, each with scattered pock marks around it. These are now filled with red resin, accentuating their pattern, as a memorial to the destruction and loss of that desperate period from 1992 to 1996. Their almost floral appearance has given them the name Sarajevo Roses. The footprints opposite the bridge have returned too with a circumspect statement on a plaque: "From this place on 28 June 1914 Gavrilo Princip assassinated the heir to the Austro-Hungarian throne Franz Ferdinand and his wife Sofia."

Most schoolchildren learn about the shots fired in Sarajevo that were the trigger for World War I even if they never entirely grasp the sequence that sparked a global conflagration. It appears unlikely that Princip and his fellow conspirators themselves anticipated the scale of what would ensue as they positioned themselves along the route of the imperial motorcade. They were Bosnian Serbs belonging to an underground revolutionary group

---

30. The account of Princip and the vagaries of the footprint memorial is based on the following: Miller, "Yugoslav Eulogies"; Slijepcevic, "Monument and Counter-Monument Sights."

Princip footprint memorial, Sarajevo. Photograph: Author, November 2022.

called Young Bosnia, which was agitating for the overthrow of Austro-Hungarian rule, and the plot was instigated partly by an associated secretive Serbian nationalist group called The Black Hand. As the open-topped car rolled up the quay, one of the conspirators lobbed a grenade. It bounced off the car and exploded behind them, injuring others. The royal party continued on to city hall. It was confusion around changes to their return journey that resulted in the car turning into the street where Princip, assuming the plot had failed, now stood. He stepped forward and from a distance of four or five paces, as he recalled it at his trial, he shot them both. The vagaries of his footprints remain one of the most idiosyncratic memorial histories of a much-memorialized war.

Looking for them in 1964 on the war's fiftieth anniversary, a *New York Times* reporter describes their casual appearance on the sidewalk, perhaps only of interest to a tourist.[31] The original footprints, he says, were from a period sketch of the assassination. The toes pointed outward, ballet fashion as if the young assassin had been posing for posterity. Princip had tried to kill himself after firing the shots but he failed. Instead, he was immediately arrested, brought to trial and sentenced to a 20-year term, since, at age nineteen, he was too young for capital punishment. He died of tuberculosis in 1918, in abject conditions at Terezin, north of Prague. Terezin was a military prison that would later become the Nazi show-concentration-camp known as Theresienstadt, spruced up to influence world opinion, most notably that of the Red Cross. Under strict instructions to bury Princip in an unmarked grave, a Czech guard kept track of the burial site. The bones were returned to Bosnia in 1920.

---

31. Barry, "Sarajevo Revisited."

In the newly constituted kingdom of Yugoslavia, Princip was seen as a hero, one who fired the first shot against Austro-Hungarian rule. Latin Bridge was renamed Princip's Bridge. The monument to Franz Ferdinand and Sophie, called the "monument of assassination" and erected on the assassination's third anniversary, was torn down in favor of commemorating Princip. During World War II, the commemorative plaque was sent to Hitler as a birthday gift. In 1953, the communist government imprinted a pair of footprints at the site to signify the spot where Princip stood. It was these prints that the *New York Times* reporter later found, together with a plaque stating that Gavrilo Princip gave expression to the nation's protest against tyranny. The West might view Princip as a terrorist, but Tito, who was Yugoslavia's leader for over twenty-five years, saw in Princip not only an anti-colonial revolutionary but a proto-socialist.

The Princip memorial was rebuilt a couple of times by the Yugoslavian state, but during the Bosnian war, the footprints were removed and the plaque changed to acknowledge the events of June 1914 in a non-committal way. Latin Bridge also took back its name. A city that had faced such a barrage of shelling from Serbian forces bore no love for any Serb, even a Bosnian one. Some observers say it was common for people to spit on the footprints or at the plaque during the 1992–1996 war. However, more than a decade later, Sarajevo was distant enough from the war for the footprints to be re-installed at the same spot outside the Museum of Sarajevo 1878-1918. The plaque simply states the facts. The museum is a single room with a few artifacts, including garments, photographs, and maps. It refers to the period of Austro-Hungarian rule as one that brought "changes," sometimes "radical changes," to socioeconomic life, architecture, culture, and economy. Outside, schoolchildren crowd around the footprints with their teacher so that their damp soles leave their own imprints all around Princip's.

The persistence of the footprints, especially their reappearance as a commemorative form on the site, is curious. Even as it cannot be like the cenotaphs and statues that elsewhere symbolize the war and its losses, it is also unlike other sidewalk memorials. In fact, as sidewalk memorials go, it lacks the shock of recognition of the Sarajevo Roses or the interruptive trip-up of the *stolpersteine*, Gunter Demnig's "stumble stones" of brass plates bearing the name and birth and death dates of victims of the Nazi extermination machine that are installed on sidewalks in Germany and beyond. Princip's footprints are easily overlooked even though they are directly outside the museum. Asphalt, the museum tells us, conscientiously serving its function of representing the Austro-Hungarian years, was first laid on a Sarajevo street in 1901. A brickyard opened more than twenty years earlier, bus service started in 1880, street lights and the electric tram arrived in 1895, in fact all the stuff we think of as building the modern city.[32] On this even surface, the royal motorcade was meant to ride smoothly and the teenage assassin planted himself in the crowd on a sidewalk we would recognize today.

Those who wish to do so can stand in his shoes and see things from his vantage point. Different efforts have been made to direct this point of view—to the anti-colonial revolutionary, the Serbian nationalist, or as a salutary reminder of violence past—and yoke it to political purposes. Princip's footprints themselves convey little about the thrust of the hip, the slump of the shoulders, or

---

32. This information was on a wall text when I visited the museum in November 2022.

the swagger of youth in a tubercular frame, to dictate its meaning. The plaque does the work of setting the tone. Which begs the question: why footprints? While statues of Princip have been installed elsewhere, at this momentous street corner, he is only marked by his feet. As these unexceptional impressions do little to convey defiance, perhaps it is that such a modest and down to earth symbol can weather changing claims, given that the sculptural vocabulary holds no innate heroism, no pre-determined prescription for how to see. And yet, the footprints have repeatedly come and gone. Might we remind ourselves then of the resilience of footprints in cities determined to obliterate them? Or marvel at a symbol that evades capture and is promiscuous about perspectives? Feet move, which is why we can follow in their footsteps. It is futile then to secure a claim to a single duck-footed stance. The prints were actually historically inaccurate: according to the newspaper report, they were made from a shoe two sizes too big. Young Gavrilo would have easily stepped out of them and disappeared into the city.

ITINERARY 4

TRACK

Unsettling

No sooner had the footprints surfaced than they had to be buried again. So many factors might imperil them: erosion by wind and water, careless human steps and animal traffic, the extremes of temperature in the area, or changes in the chemical composition of their substrate. That they dated to 20,000 years ago would have been a miraculous discovery in itself had the region not already demonstrated that there was continual human presence dating back another 20,000 years earlier. In the 1970s, human remains that were ritually cremated and interred had been unearthed, of a man and a woman who have come to be known as Mungo Man and Mungo Lady. To the Paakantji, Mutthi Mutthi, and Ngyiampaa people of the country, who had never doubted that their peoples had always been there, it was external validation of their uninterrupted connection to the place.[1]

---

1. The account of the Willandra footprints is drawn from the following: McGrath, "People of the Footprints;" Webb et al, "Pleistocene Human Footprints."

Pintupi trackers, invited down to flesh out an understanding of these footprints, recognized that this was *tjukurrpa*, a term typically translated as "dreamtime," dating from the period when ancestors were creating the world. The Pintupi were from the Central Desert in the Northern Territory of Australia, where their skills in the art and science of understanding the landscape had been finely honed. Speaking through an interpreter, they drew a story out of these marks. Over a span of many seasons, various family groups of all ages had traversed the area, sometimes walking beside each other, sometimes meandering on their own. They pointed out a woman probably carrying a baby on her hip and there, a child who wandered away from the group and circled back, nervous at being left behind or summoned by a parent. Men hunted kangaroo. One man threw his spear, missed and then speared once more in a final thrust. They could identify where the spear had been thrown only to ricochet off the surface or where someone rested a spear with the blunt end down on the ground or where sticks and branches had been dragged to build a fire. A child, budding artist or bored, had scratched a doodle on the ground.

Using biomechanical analysis, scientists could discern that some of the men were tall, well over six feet, athletic, with running speeds approaching today's Olympic standards, but they had been flummoxed by a series of right feet that had no left counterpart. Perhaps the site had been a shallow pond, and the person was in a dugout canoe poling with one leg. No, the Pintupi thought it was a man with one leg, severed substantially above the foot so that he wasn't dragging its stump. He may have used a stick for support, but it was likely that at some point he flung it aside and was leaping almost three feet at a time, as springy as a pogo stick, with his one leg alone. The trackers knew a one-legged man in their own village so they could spot the patterns. Had these tracks been made recently back home, they would probably have been able to name every individual. And thus, the picture emerges of a gathering place, which lakesides so often are, of human and animal, men and women, emus and marsupials, children with adults, walking together, running and hunting, exploring. Measurements and scientific analyses had sketched in outline the bodies to go with the feet, but the trackers infused the bodies with vitality.

Willandra Lakes, where these forebears gathered, is a semi-arid region in the Far West of New South Wales in Australia. At the time when the footprints were made, it was home to a substantial lake system, but it is now a landscape of some scrub, grassland and woodland, extensive sand dunes, and ancient dried lake beds. As the wind comes in from the southwest, the sand is blown off the dunes so that they begin to move. Called lunettes because of their crescent shape, these dunes have migrated northward so that footprints that had been blanketed by sand were gradually exposed. The once moist soil by the lakes was the perfect receiving ground for a squelching foot to leave an imprint complete with individual toes, heel and ball, but it was probably a rolling sandstorm blowing soon after to cover it that sealed its place for posterity. Since the first print, about seven hundred footprints have come to light in roughly twenty-five individual trackways of four or more prints, drying in the clay almost like concrete. In the restless landscape of the dunes, it is possible that more footprints might surface.

The first of these footprints was identified in 2003. This was followed, in 2006, by extensive excavation of the multiple trackways of prints, after which it was felt that the footprints could not be subjected to casual exposure. Several options were considered to shelter and protect them.[2] Conservators from the Getty Institute in the U.S. who had worked on the reburial of the Laetoli hominin footprints in Tanzania came in to consult on the matter. Finally, the archaeologists, conservators, and scientists as well as the National Parks and Wildlife Service, working with the Aboriginal Advisory Group for Willandra Lakes, determined that these prints too should be reburied. Local sand was poured back in and covered with a synthetic shade textile held down by sandbags. This mimicked the lunettes that had once held the footprints while preventing the ongoing movement that had exposed them. These accidental but persistent footprints have been scanned, molded in rubber and made into concrete tiles so that they are eternally visible to visitors to the park.[3]

There is a pressure on footprints to show themselves. It is part of their power and seduction that footprints can stake a claim by making presences visible. Once they're revealed, it's hard to let them go, even prompting a desire to fix them. Yet the world to which the footprints at this relict lakeside bear testimony is far from immutable. Once formed in the chemical wizardry of sand, water, and clay, the footprints surface from below, conjured into the present by the same sand, wind, and water, manifesting a restive and unsettled planet. Here, feet mill around, walking both together and alone, working and whiling away time, where a child may take one small independent step. And it is only by perceiving them in the fullness of their lively movement that a one-legged

---

2. Macgregor, "Preserving the Ancient Human Trackways Site."
3. See Mungo National Park website: https://visitmungo.com.au/footprint-replicas.html

man from the Pleistocene might make a giant leap not only into the world of our present but beyond.

Foundation

The propensity of footprints to acquire definition makes them singularly persuasive artifacts. Around the time the prints surfaced in Willandra Lakes, other footprints on a watery foreshore in Arnhem Land in Australia's Northern Territory were about to demonstrate their presence. To see these footprints required no small knowledge and insight. The Yolngu people of the area intended to assert their claim to an intertidal zone, that area between low and high tides, where the water flowed over their land. They were no strangers to the land rights movement. In 1963, confronted with a lease being granted to a bauxite mine on their territory, without any consultation, they had sent a petition to the government to recognize their rights. In 2003, they were seeking to establish "sea rights" as part of a title claim. The Blue Mud Bay decision, as it is called, finally determined by the High Court in 2008, was a landmark in recognizing Yolngu title over this zone of land and water.

The genesis of this case was the intrusion of a fishing party into a site among the mangroves of Blue Mud Bay considered sacred by the Yolngu. The area was home to Bäru, the ancestral crocodile and a nesting ground for the saltwater species. Bits of trash, bedding, and fuel containers were scattered about the camp and a bag held the severed head of a crocodile. Stung by the desecration, forty-seven Yolngu artists were prompted to express what these places meant to them and the sense of injury that such actions evoked. They created a series of eighty bark paintings to demonstrate the philosophy, law, rules, and stories that link Yolngu people to the coasts, rivers, and oceans. Collectively called the Saltwater Collection, an exhibition of these paintings toured around the country seeking to communicate Yolngu understanding of sea country to outsiders.[4] Some of these paintings—that of Bäru the crocodile, of ancestral hunters in canoes hunting dugongs, and of the stingray found in shallow waters—were submitted to the court and entered into evidence in the Blue Mud Bay case.[5]

These paintings manifest Yolngu *djalkiri*, a word that literally means foot, footprint, or step but in its encapsulation of philosophy, interrelationship, identity, and law, signifies the foundation of the Yolngu way of life. Their country is shaped by ancestors who, as they traversed land and water, left their traces in djalkiri. Djalkiri is not the residue of a former time, not just the imprints of those who have gone. As the Gay'wu Group of Women, or the "dilly bag women's group" of five Yolngu sisters with non-Yolngu collaborators, describe it, djalkiri emerges from the soil, giving them their tongue, the words to speak.[6] As the ancestor is transferred into each part of the environment—rocks, landscape features, waters, living beings—not only is the place born but all in it are made together as if of one substance. Humans, animals, and plants are inextricably incorporated and emplaced. Djalkiri is a foundation because it provides guidance, the law, rules for living that tell humans how to know the world around them and how to be in it with others. Because it binds humans to a place, the law is conceived as following in the footsteps of ancestors in ways that are continually kept alive through songs, paintings, dances, and

---

4. The Saltwater paintings are now in the collection of the Australian National Maritime Museum in Sydney.
5. Carrick, "Art, Law and the Yolngu People of East Arnhem Land."
6. Gay'wu Group of Women, *Song Spirals*. Also see Tamisari, "Body, Vision and Movement."

stories. The visible manifestations in the landscape exude ancestral power but they may also appear through sound, smell, touch, and dreams.

Presenting a footprint so that it can provide evidence in a legal argument or indeed scientific evidence of long-standing presence is tricky even when necessary. The footprint must become a fixed object, a document that can be deployed in a courtroom to make a claim to occupation, to residence, to ownership. The Yolngu have grown experienced in the need to make apparent their imprinted and entangled world in the secular contexts of law, science, and art. Since the 1930s, they have been making paintings on stringy bark, drawing clan designs, illuminating an intertwined environment of land, sea, and sky with braided lineages of human and animal to anthropologists and art collectors, missionaries and judges, politicians and administrators. Many of these paintings originally would have been on the bodies of initiates or dancers but began to be made on eucalyptus bark.[7] Djambawa Marawili, an artist and clan leader who was the instigator of the Saltwater education campaign, has said of Yolngu painting practices that the "patterns and designs are beneath" and that they "lift the art from the country" to make it strong.[8]

Among the most significant communal Yolngu works are church panels painted in 1962-63 as a multi-clan response to the threat of bauxite mining. They are installed in a mission church at Yirrkala, an area whose sovereignty had already been appropri-

---

7. See the catalogue of a landmark 2024 exhibition: Wanambi et al, *Madayin*. Also see Geissler, "Contemporary Indigenous Australian Art and Native Title Land Claim."

8. Marawili, Djambawa, "Introduction" in Nomad Art Productions, "Djalkiri."

ated by the Australian state. Petitions on bark that asserted their rights through clan designs and in text written both in Gumatj, a Yolngu language, and English, were sent to the Parliament at the same time. They also took the federal government and the mining company to court. The case was unsuccessful. It was evident to the judge that their customary law demonstrated a relationship to land, but it was still insufficient to meet legal definitions embedded in European conceptions of property—as such, the land was considered *terra nullius*, nobody's land, free for the taking. Nonetheless, the bark petitions are displayed in Parliament as the inaugural act of the land rights movement in Australia.

Crusoe's Dreaming

A footprint is an open invitation. Imagine that the print of a human foot appears on a seashore. It might so easily wash away in the next great surge in a high wind, but it stays on as one of the most renowned images of English literature. This unshod foot was found by Daniel Defoe's Robinson Crusoe, a slave trader who became a castaway for decades on a remote island. Crusoe is struck dumb by the sight: a single footprint, without its partner. He listens, he looks around, he walks up and down, he looks again in case he imagined it but there it is, the "print of a Foot, Toes, Heel and every Part of a Foot."[9] Without Pintupi trackers to explain how a single footprint might come to be, he flees.

Crusoe has spent his long years of isolation turning loneliness into industry. He planted fields, hunted birds and fish, made pastures and pens, kept goats, taught a parrot to speak, established

9. Defoe, *Robinson Crusoe*, 112.

rules and laws, erected a cross, built fortifications and enclosures, to create a reclusive domain that has inspired and instructed generations of readers in its heady mix of fortitude, independence, wilderness, and mastery. By the time the footprint appears, the castaway, initially almost wild in his terror and abandonment, has "re-civilized" himself.

With its appearance, his carefully balanced world begins to teeter. Was the footprint that of the Devil, he wonders. How else would a single print appear with no other marks or signs of human presence? Or even more dangerous than the Devil—savages in canoes coming over from the mainland to enact the worst rituals of cannibalism? Were they to return, they would surely devour him or destroy his well-wrought world with its enclosures of corn and goats. He had longed to see other humans but now, this unmistakable sign of one terrified him. Wait! Might it just be an imprint of his own foot? The relief! He can't recall ever being on that bit of shoreline, but he returns to measure it. No, there can be no doubt. The foot is larger than his own. Crusoe retreats into a feverish anxiety of fortification—he finds new redoubts in caves, ceases to light a fire lest the smoke be seen, builds barriers and bulwarks of plants, timber, and cable—simultaneously haunted and hunted by the footprint.

There are stray moments of reprieve. He is aware of his unfounded suspicions about the "savages." A moral sanity prevails—these people had done him no harm. Who was he to pass judgement on their practices or to try to kill them? It would be indefensible, tantamount to murder. Almost two decades have gone by without him ever having spotted another human being or being spotted by a passing ship so why should this footprint awaken such fear? Time rolls on. No answers are forthcoming.

Once, he sees the "savage" mainlanders on the shore and hides. At another point, a ship founders on the rocks but everyone on it has perished except for a dog. The years pass relentlessly until in a dream, he sees himself rescuing a prisoner from the cannibals, turning him into a servant who would act as his pilot and bring him back to the mainland.

Is this a premonition of what is to happen or a subconscious pre-determination of how he would handle the next human sighting, the one he was most likely to see? When the canoes do finally alight again on the shore, Crusoe is prepared for them, although it is surely chance that one of the prisoners makes a run for it. He rescues the man from his pursuers. In gratitude and relief, the man kisses the ground, lays his head upon it, takes Crusoe's foot and sets it upon his head. In this gesture, Crusoe sees that the man has sworn to be his slave forever. He names him Friday for the day of their meeting. Crusoe recognizes the footprint now and it is indeed his own.

Much ink has been spilled in characterizing this encounter, archetypally colonial with its willful exploitation of another human being in a homesteading paranoia. Far less has been said about the footprint itself. Many analyses assume that the footprint is Friday's, even though many years elapse between its appearance and his, or they presume that it might as well be Friday's, as if Crusoe's colonial dreamtime had transmogrified the foot at its first sighting. The text itself offers no explanation as to whose footprint it might be. Think about it again: a single footprint on a wet beach. Under what conditions would it appear, while wiping its partner out completely? If there is no one on the island, as Crusoe's subsequent patrols suggest, who could have imprinted it on the shore with such firm definition? Could the footprint have surfaced on its own, up from below as they sometimes do, in an alchemy of sand, wind and water? Stay for a minute with that image before its identity and meaning are foreclosed. When he encountered it, Crusoe himself vacillated between fear and familiarity, between perceived malevolence and possible identification. Was the island not filled with a mess of prints in which his own could be found alongside those of goats, cats, birds and reptiles? A single footprint only had to look to this teeming life for its partner.

Tracking

The castaway longed for a guide to lead him out. This was the person who knew nobody's land better than anybody and who was ready to lay his knowledge at the feet of the intrepid explorer. When exploration gave way to settlement, the guide gave way to the tracker, soon pressed into service by colonial police. In 1819, J.T. Bigge, the commissioner appointed to assess the administration of the New South Wales government, wrote of Aboriginal trackers in his report: "by extraordinary strength of sight that they possess, improved by their daily exercise of it in pursuit of kangaroos and opossums, they can trace with wonderful accuracy, the impressions of the human foot."[10] The new Australian penal colony regularly employed "black trackers" to hunt down fugitive white convicts, recover wandering livestock or property, track lost settlers or to serve as guides.

No formal unit was established. Instead, trackers were recruited locally, as and when needed, and were typically paid in kind with flour, maize, axes, clothing, or blankets rather than with cash. That the list was reasonable recompense signals the ways in

---

10. Quoted in Blyton, "Black Trackers," 61.

which the self-sufficiency of the communities to which these men belonged was being destroyed. There is nothing on record to tell us what the trackers felt about this work, but their deployment and efficacy sparked anger and hostility from the white prisoners desperate for their freedom and often themselves victims of poverty and disregard. Trackers were rarely mentioned by name in any documents even when these included admiring accounts of how they could track an "ant over a rock." [11]

Through the nineteeth and early twentieth centuries, the colonies were the laboratories for technologies of surveillance and identification—like fingerprinting, footprinting, and dog-tracking—as well as anthropometric classifications that shaped conceptions of race and eugenics. For the burgeoning forensic practices in criminology, trackers were invaluable—nothing seemed to escape them, whether it was slightly disturbed earth, insects where they shouldn't be, or a snagged twig. In 1851, the Sydney Morning Herald marveled at the Aboriginal trackers: "Like the American Indians, they can go from one place to another in a straight line, without any track or even the sun to guide them."[12] Both the native tracker and the literary detective owe their mystique to this time. Today's ubiquitous harvesting of biometric data by police and border regimes is done by automated systems, but the legacy of the discerning eye hasn't altogether vanished.

In 1974, the U.S. Congress established a Native American unit in the Tohono O'odham nation on the U.S.- Mexico border. The ancestral territories of the Tohono O'odham span both sides of the border, whose fencing cuts through miles of their nation. The tactical patrol unit, called Shadow Wolves, works in the Sonoran

11. Ibid, 64.
12. Ibid, 66

Desert, where it intercepts human and drug smugglers. The cardinal feature of the group is its members' ability to "cut for sign," that is, to follow a track based on physical evidence such as footprints, tire tracks, fragments of clothing, fiber, or hair. "Sign" refers to this evidence and "cutting" means being able to spot and analyze it. Observers of their tracking patrols remark on the uncanny awareness of these trackers—they can tell when someone has rested a bale on the ground, the difference between old and recent footprints from the way in which tracks of animals and birds interact with them, or when the track is that of migrants whose light trace betrays how little they're carrying, and shuffle marks are a tell-tale sign that the person has turned around to look, aware that they're being pursued. According to ICE (Immigration and Customs Enforcement), the unit was named because they hunt in a pack like wolves.[13] This animalized machismo permeates the accounts. An article in *Smithsonian Magazine* calls it "today's hunt;" another journalist refers to them as catching "their prey."[14] One of the Shadow Wolves officers himself says, "If one wolf finds prey, it will call in the rest of the pack."[15]

In 1970, not long before the Shadow Wolves were instituted, the Israeli Defense Force (IDF) established the Bedouin Tracker Unit. As guides, some Bedouin had worked with the British as well as with the Palmach, the elite unit of the underground Jewish army during the British Mandate in Palestine. Some had also served as guides to the Turks and Egyptians at various times, managing relationships with all powers that intruded into their

---

13. US Immigration and Customs Enforcement, "ICE Shadow Wolves," www.ice.gov, n.d.

14. See Wheeler, "Shadow Wolves;"; Vanderpool, "Native Trackers."

15. Wheeler, 40.

A Shadow Wolves agent examines a mark near the Tohono O'odham Reservation, Arizona, in May 2002. © Scott Warren. Courtesy: Imago.

lands. In 2005, artist Ahlam Shibli created a series called *Trackers*, consisting of eighty-five color and black and white photographs depicting young Bedouin men who volunteer for the tracker unit of the IDF.[16] The images show gangly young men with camouflage face paint undergoing military training. They shoulder weapons, one walks away from the camera with a grenade, another lies flat looking through a scope, they huddle for instructions. But most of the photographs catch the men as if off-stage—three of them together clean weapons, one scratches a bit of graffiti at the corner of the image, they lean on one another in casual camaraderie, resting and waiting, reading, smoking, or in single portraits with mouths slightly open as if in anticipation of adulthood.

16. Szymczyk, ed., *Ahlam Shibli Trackers*.

Yet this is not about everyday routines of military life for callow recruits, nor an indictment of the choice being made by men in a state hostile to their presence. Shibli herself is a Palestinian of Bedouin descent who presently holds an Israeli passport. Clear-eyed as the images are, they are drained of drama. They resist the compulsion to persuade. Without thrill but without anger either. They are also devoid of tracks, traces, footmarks. It is the viewer who must cut for sign. One set of photographs catches the men on leave, standing in uniform by their seated mothers and aunts or crouched with a cup of tea as an older man smokes a cigarette. Behind them are half-finished buildings, or houses with simple corrugated roofs. A road winds past scattered dwellings and in front of a scrubby hillock where cattle graze, a man stands in uniform, hands on hips, looking into the distance.

Bedouin have been largely sedentarized even if the tracker unit is drawing on the traditional skills of nomadic groups seeking water and pasture for their flocks.[17] Tracking is daily life for the herder or hunter following the prints of hoofs and pads in sand, forest, snow, and ice. The job of the Bedouin trackers is mainly reconnaissance and tracking those who trespass even as they themselves have become trespassers on the lands their forebears once traversed but to which they held no recognizable legal title. Many live in villages unrecognized by the state which frequently have no basic services, where they are not allowed to build permanent structures. Volunteering for the army is one way to improve their situation, as it permits them to buy land and build houses. Inside these houses, Shibli shows us, families hang pictures of the young men in uniform.

---

17. Ginat, "How a Bedouin Tracker Sees the Desert."

Ahlam Shibli, untitled (*Trackers* no. 21), Palestine/Israel, 2005, gelatin silver print, 37x55.5 cm. © Ahlam Shibli. Courtesy of the artist.

Marks on the ground are only the trace of a story. Where a footprint once unlocked a world of co-inhabitants, it is now the key to locking it from both trespass and desecration. The need for a footprint to be proof, to secure a claim, to offer a leg to stand on in the face of social, political, and ecological precarity has erased the open-endedness of a footprint's question. When the Gay'wu women keen the whale songline, it's about sitting there, being on the boat, going along, singing about the spirit's final journey, travelling for the last time, watching the whales out on the ocean.[18] A pastoralist takes her cue from the restlessness of the herd ready to leave for cooler greening pastures.[19] One of the Shadow Wolves describes learning skills from his grandfather, who taught him to listen to the desert, to pay attention to sounds.[20] The charisma of footprints has congealed as evidence. The narrative of its allure, the way it entices and compels both the curious and the weary, is now being written by global surveillance regimes, whether Frontex or Google.

We're still making footprints, dropping the crumbs of our cookies, finding that as we go round and round, the footprints begin to track us as they did one day with Pooh and Piglet in Hundred Acre Wood.[21] It was Pooh who was first going around tracking prints in the snow, wondering what he would find when he caught up with it, and then Piglet saw him. Now Piglet, you must remember, lived in a grand house in a beech tree under the sign "Trespassers W," which was his grandfather's name. But now

---

18. Gay'wu Group of Women, *Song Spirals*, Chapter 1.
19. See Gooch, "Feet Following Hooves" In Ingold and Vergunst, *Ways of Walking*.
20. Vanderpool, op. cit.
21. Milne and Shepard, *Winnie-The-Pooh*, Chapter III.

Pooh and Piglet following the possible tracks of a Woozle. Illustration by E.H. Shepard from Winnie the Pooh (1926) by A. A. Milne. Public domain, via Wikimedia Commons.

he was only clearing things at his front door when he saw Pooh and decided to walk over to see what was going on. When he saw the tracks, Piglet was afraid it was a Woozle and so it could be, said Pooh, or it couldn't; you never could tell with pawmarks.

And off they went and isn't that the thing about walking and thinking: you can do it on your own or even when you're walking with a friend, and isn't it wonderful to chat about grandfathers and health and everything under the sun and nothing at all with a friend in the sunshine in the woods or around the trees. Any walker will tell you that there are times when you know that it is your legs that direct your brain, that your weighty head is merely a puppet of your stride, yanked by the strings so that as you walk, ideas tumble in and whoosh out, and a bit of song comes into your head to go with the rhythm of your feet and the swinging choreography of your arms. But even as they went along together, Pooh and Piglet found that the footprint tracks were multiplying and beginning to follow them. Many Woozles was a scary proposition so they were thankful when Christopher Robin came to their rescue. Piglet could return to his beech tree house, which he later gave up when Owl's home was destroyed in a wind and trespassers w or not, Owl needed a welcome. But that's another story.

Migration and Memory

Stories migrate too along with feet. They carry the memories of our anxieties and adventures, but they also carry the pleasures and fears of what we left behind, of what drove us out and propels us onward. Like the time when the rabbits cursed the tracks of the mighty elephants. This is a nomadic tale that began somewhere in the Panchatantra fables of India, making its way through the Persian into the Arabic Kalila wa Dimna and from there into He-

"The Clever Hare with the King of the Elephants at the Spring of the Moon." Folio from a Kalila wa Dimna, second quarter of the sixteenth century, Gujarat, India. Probably based on an Egyptian version. Ink and opaque watercolor on paper. Creative Commons license (CC0), original work at the Metropolitan Museum, New York.

brew, Greek, and Old Castilian. This is the story.[22] The drought had been unrelenting. Tanks, ponds, swamps, and lakes had all run dry. The forest was as tinder. The elephants had been seeking water for twelve years but the earth was parched. Their great king, he of the four tusks, could stand it no longer. He sent scouts out in eight directions in search of water while they waited. Finally, there was news—near a hermitage was the lake of the moon.

A lake such as this you haven't seen in your wildest imagination. A shady leafy paradise, where the trees bow deeply on its banks, where ospreys, ducks, cranes, and herons dip into its waters, languid with lotuses and waterlilies. The herd dared not hope as they journeyed eastward to the lake but yes, there it was as it had been described. Deranged with thirst, they plunged into its waters, drinking, cavorting, soaking their sun-scorched bodies, easing the memories of these many rainless years. But as they rushed into the lake, they hadn't noticed the colonies of rabbits who lived on its banks, unwittingly crushing many under the press of their heavy feet. The rabbits gathered in the aftermath of this massacre. They could see the elephant tracks, which only meant the herd would be back.

As they wailed and cursed, one crafty long-eared fellow said he had an idea, which he would share if they would appoint him their ambassador. The grateful rabbit king sent him off. The rabbit reached the herd on their way back to the lake—thousands of grey ears waving like monsoon clouds, tusks like flashes of white lightning, trumpeting like thunder in their anticipation. The rabbit climbed onto a mound for a bit of courage and so he could be seen. He humbly greeted the old four-tusker, introducing himself as an

---

22. "How the Rabbit Fooled the Elephant." In Ryder, *The Panchatantra*, 308–15.

envoy and asking that no harm come to him. He had been sent by the lady of the lake, the moon, who commanded him to tell the elephants that they had desecrated her sanctity. In entering the lake with such little regard, they had slaughtered the rabbits under her protection. Don't you know about the rabbit in the moon? he asked. If the elephants stop, the lady commanded him to say, they will be bathed in moonlight. If they continue, they will be scorched by heat and perish.

The elephant king was horrified and chastened. What can we do? he asked. Come alone at night, said the rabbit. The lake was even more beautiful in the moonlit night. The whirring of night insects, the plop of fish, the occasional frog's croak. The moon was reflected in the water, a beautiful quivering disc, surrounded by the planets and stars of the heavenly firmament. The old king was overwhelmed. He wanted to purify himself and worship her. He dipped his huge trunk into the lake to draw up water. Ripples rushed furiously across the lake so that you could see a thousand moons. Stop, stop, cried the rabbit, you have enraged the moon! Why? asked the troubled elephant. Because you touched her waters, said the rabbit. Forgive us, said the elephant, and the herd retreated, never to return.

This story of the rabbit's wily trickery is usually told as an instance of how he outwitted the great elephant. And certainly, we can see in it the ingenuity and survival skills of small folk trodden under the merciless feet of giant forces. But is it also an old story of a changing climate's terrible impact on multiple lives? Climbing temperatures and decreased rainfall will demonstrate their greatest impacts on species like the elephant, which only stand at the apex of a cascade of other species that will be ravaged by drought, wildfires, heat, and stress.[23] And as these conditions worsen, will these populations not seek relief elsewhere? If the story cautions us that those deranged by terrible devastation cannot trample others in their search for survival, it also raises the question of whether prevailing under such conditions is inherently unequal and only possible by virtue of duplicity. Must the elephants be condemned to a dry death so that the rabbits survive? Or is there another way to share the bounty of the earth under the silver moon?

Eluding Capture

There are five reflecting panels on the moon that date back to our first steps there, half a century ago. Each of them is made of a hundred mirrors, called "corner cubes" by scientists, that reflect light back to any direction it comes from. The astronauts of Apollo 11 delivered two in 1969 during the first moonwalks and more were dropped off in later missions. It is the last working science experiment of this early era of space exploration and it's a simple one: Aim a beam of light and measure the time it takes for it to bounce back—which is 2.5 seconds. Four telescopes, located in Italy, France, Germany, and New Mexico in the U.S., fire lasers at these corner cubes for this calculation. But it's not as you might imagine, just a beam of light shooting out from Earth to the moon. Earth's thick atmosphere scatters the photons as they leave and scatters them again on the way back. It's a one in 25 million chance that a photon will get to the moon and one in 250 million that one will make it back.[24]

The biggest revelation of this experiment is that the earth

---

23. International Fund for Animal Welfare (IFAW), "The Impact of Climate Change on Elephants."
24. For this account of the relationship between the moon and earth, see Jet Propulsion Laboratory (JPL), "The Apollo Experiment That Keeps on Giving;" Steigerwald, "Laser Beams Reflected between Earth and Moon."

Laser ranging retroreflector deployed by Apollo 14 astronauts. February 5, 1971. Courtesy: NASA

and moon are drifting apart at the rate of 1.5 inches or 3.8 centimeters a year—which is apparently the rate that fingernails grow. This is because of the gravitational interaction between the two bodies, the very energies that cause the tidal movements central to the rhythm of the Earth. The moon is made up of remnants of Earth. This has made it a scientific goldmine for understanding the youth of our own planet, including possibly the genesis of life. The bold footprints that once left the earth and entered our imagination, that seemed to be permanently captured by the airless moon, will one day leave our orbit forever. Our greatest memorialization is spinning away from us into the future even as it carries with it the hopes we had in the past. But all around us, footprints are surfacing from below, if we knew how to see them. If only we paid less attention to preserving these footprints and more to conserving the worlds that brought them into being. The past and the future are in the now of the footprint. Can you see it?

GUIDEPOST

Tibetan monks in the twelfth century could request the footprints of their preceptors on cloth; being in contact with these imprints in meditation was as sound as the voice of a teacher. In the print, the teacher's presence, imbued in a piece of cloth, can travel across generations. The imprint offered both injunction and possibility, guidance and independence. However, it was not an intellectual pedagogic signifier but a visceral experience that was simultaneously tactile, sonic, and material. This footprint is not an inert carrier; it is an elemental encounter. The encounter it promises is a mystery but it is not mystifying. Its charge rests in the relationship it awakens between the mentor's presence and the monk's quest. Even as the desire might arise to hold the footprint as an object of contemplation, even a touchstone, the monk is aware that the preceptor's feet will not substitute for the hard tramp of one's own journey.

The ground of these journeys may be covered with bold and easy strides or in a cautious, measured pace; they demand persistence, that one trudge without flagging; and in human and animal alike, travel leaves tracks, tracing a rough path that others may follow. No one fails to leave a mark and our world is alive with them.

How to relate to the liveliness of footprints surrounding us has been the question driving the journeys in this book. It was as a walker that I came to them. That is, the questions originated in my feet rather than in my head. The imperative of their errantry is that feet and their prints have resisted any narrow analytic predisposition. They have reminded me that the footprint is born of the whisper of the foot on the ground, thoroughly palpable yet buoyant with potential. It is not entirely stable in the present nor in the past but can be continually encountered anew.

The footprint is a metaphor too, one that sets alight our imaginations; yet, of late, this flame has frequently died out in the embers of a single all-encompassing meaning that only preserves the footprint as an artifact of impact and occupation. The itineraries in this book have sought to reveal that the moment we sedentarize its metaphors, we have left our feet far behind. This has implications for how we characterize the rights and virtues of stability over mobilities, and how we conceptualize the relationships of itinerancy to belonging. The foot has been circumspect but it's rarely idle and, consequently, its history and imagery have been restless. It would be a mistake to restrain its identity and adjudicate its contradictions into a single indictment or confirmation—and equally to pit interpretations against one another to champion a new footprint for our times. Instead, can we hold the footprint open, as the monks might, as an invitation to enter into a journey, even a relationship, full of rigors but not prescribed? If you are ready, ask yourself: how will I greet my next step?

ACKNOWLEDGMENTS

I am indebted to the Multiple Mobilities Research Group ("the Mob")—Victoria Hattam, Laura Y. Liu, Miriam Ticktin, and Rafi Youatt—with whom so many steps were first taken, for their unfailing insights, plentiful humor, and many individual acts of support.

For the back and forth of ideas and laughter that have given both buoyancy and heft to every journey herein and much more besides, I am profoundly thankful to Pradeep Dalal, Julia Foulkes, Terike Haapoja, Lydia Matthews, and Silvia Rocciolo.

To artists Mona Hatoum, Ahlam Shibli, and Birender Yadav, my gratitude for their responsiveness and the use of their images—and to Birender additionally for the largesse with which he shared his experiences. Phillip and Judy Tuwaletstiwa provided generous and generative perspectives. Conversations with Bill Gilbert have been companions on these walks. Carin Kuoni and Aleksandra Wagner furthered my delight through transcontinental memories of inexpensive footwear. To Aleksandra additionally, my special gratitude for the rich introduction to Sarajevo. Thanks to Sara Morawetz for a stimulating conversation about her performative walk *étalon* retracing the measurement of the meter; and to Smita Shukla for the window into prosthetic fit.

Despite or perhaps because of its periodic tumult, my professional home, Parsons School of Design/The New School, has provided a hospitable environment for interdisciplinary research and practice, for which I am deeply appreciative. I thank my many colleagues who never fail to engage with openness and enthusiasm, thereby sustaining the petri dish of this culture.

The Zolberg Institute for Migration and Mobility at The New School, under director Alex Aleinikoff, provided essential funding during the research for this book, for which I am grateful.

For the invitations and opportunities to present versions of this work, I thank: Rui Filipe Antunes, Clara Gari, Terike Haapoja, Isabel Hofmeyr, Sarah Nuttall, Daniel Tércio, Geert Vermeire, and Yannis Ziogas.

Itinerary 1 was first published, with minor differences, in the journal *Borderlands* in a special issue on intersecting mobilities, edited by Miriam Ticktin and Rafi Youatt.

I am grateful to the editorial collective of EtCH, especially Neferti Tadiar and Cynthia Franklin, for the sympathetic reception to the project; and to Tim Roberts of np: for shepherding me through the publication process.

To those whose tracks are inextricable from mine and whose illumination and support have boosted many a flagging step, my thanks overflow: Yvette Christiansë, John Krawchuk, Ranjani Mazumdar, Rosalind C. Morris, and Vinnie Petrarca.

And for their imprint on life's journey, to Padmini Subramaniam and the late V. Subramaniam, incalculable gratitude.

BIBLIOGRAPHY

9/11 Memorial and Museum. "Tribute in Light | National September 11 Memorial & Museum." www.911memorial.org, n.d. https://www.911memorial.org/visit/memorial/tribute-light.

Alder, Ken. *The Measure of All Things*. Simon and Schuster. Kindle, 2014.

Archer, Michael, Guy Brett, Catherine De Zegher, and Mona Hatoum. *Mona Hatoum*. London, New York: Phaidon Press, 1997.

Armstrong, Neil A. "Neil A. Armstrong Oral History 19 September 2001. By Stephen E. Ambrose and Douglas Brinkley." Accessed April 15, 2019. https://historycollection.jsc.nasa.gov/JSCHistoryPortal/history/oral_histories/ArmstrongNA/ArmstrongNA_9-19-01.htm

Arya, A. P., and L. Klenerman. "The Jaipur Foot." *The Journal of Bone and Joint Surgery. British Volume* 90-B, no. 11 (November 2008): 1414–21.

Barahamin, Andre. "Kendeng against Cement | MR Online." March 27, 2017. https://mronline.org/2017/03/27/kendeng-against-cement/.

Barnard, Anne. "The 9/11 Tribute Lights Are Endangering 160,000 Birds a Year." *New York Times*, September 9, 2019.

Barry, Joseph. "Sarajevo Revisited, 50 Years After." *New York Times*, June 28, 1964, sec. Archives.

Beattie, Donald A. *Taking Science to the Moon: Lunar Experiments and the Apollo Program*. Baltimore, London: Johns Hopkins University Press, 2003.

Benjamin, Walter. *The Arcades Project*. Edited by Howard Eiland and

Michael Jennings. Cambridge, MA: The Belknap Press of Harvard University Press, 1999.

Bennett, M. R., J. W.K. Harris, B. G. Richmond, D. R. Braun, E. Mbua, P. Kiura, D. Olago, et al. "Early Hominin Foot Morphology Based on 1.5-Million-Year-Old Footprints from Ileret, Kenya." *Science* 323, no. 5918 (February 27, 2009): 1197–1201.

Bennett, Megan. "After 20 Years, Has Mystery of Oñate's Foot Been Solved." *New York Times*, October 20, 2017.

Benzecry, Claudio. *The Perfect Fit*. Chicago: University of Chicago Press, 2022.

Blyton, Greg. "Black Trackers: Labour Contributions of Aboriginal People in the Hunter Region of New South Wales, 1804–54." *Labour History* 114 (2018): 53–67.

Boslough, Mark. "Is the Moon House an American Stonehenge." *Astronomy Magazine*, July 2017, 51–55.

Branch, Jordan. *The Cartographic State*. Cambridge: Cambridge University Press, 2013.

Brooke, James. "Conquistador Statue Stirs Hispanic Pride and Indian Rage." *New York Times*, February 9, 1998, sec. U.S.

Candelaria, Esteban. "A Ceremony Re-Dedicating an Oñate Statue in Espanola Has Apparently Been Postponed." *Albuquerque Journal*, November 8, 2023.

Candraningrum, Dewi. "Forget Kendeng Not." *Heinrich Boell Stiftung, Southeast Asia* (blog), April 19, 2023. https://th.boell.org/en/2023/04/24/forget-kendeng-not.

Carrick, Damien. "Art, Law and the Yolngu People of East Arnhem Land," August 17, 2009. https://www.abc.net.au/listen/programs/lawreport/art-law-and-the-yolngu-people-of-east-arnhemland/3128124.

CBS News. "NASA May Not Have Televised the First Moon Landing If It Weren't for a Group of Geologists." www.cbsnews.com, May 11, 2019.

CemNet.com: The home of International Cement Review. "Indonesia Remains Gripped by Cement Overcapacity." *International Cement Review*, August 11, 2023. https://www.cemnet.com/News/story/175339/indonesia-remains-gripped-by-cement-overcapacity.html.

Colwell-Chanthaponh, Chip, and T. J. Ferguson. "Memory Pieces and Footprints: Multivocality and the Meanings of Ancient Times and

Ancestral Places among the Zuni and Hopi." *American Anthropologist* 108, no. 1 (March 2006): 148–62.

Conway, Rebecca J. *Djalkiri*. Sydney: Sydney University Press, 2021.

Davis, Lennard. "Introduction: Normality, Power and Culture." In *The Disability Studies Reader*, edited by Lennard Davis, 1–14, 2013.

De Simone, Daniel V., and Charles F. Treat. "A History of the Metric System Controversy in the United States." Gaithersburg, MD: National Bureau of Standards, Special Publication 345–410, 1971.

Defoe, Daniel. *Robinson Crusoe: An Authoritative Text, Contexts, Criticism*. Edited by Michael Shinagel. Second Edition. 1719. Reprint, New York: Norton, 1994.

DeMello, Margo. *Feet and Footwear: A Cultural Encyclopedia*. Santa Barbara, Calif.: Greenwood Press/Abc-Clio, 2009.

Dennis, Michael E. "The Measure of All Things after 2022: Ending the Era of the U.S. Survey Foot," August 19, 2021. https://events.tti.tamu.edu/conference/virtual-uesi-texas-2021-annual-conference/program/.

Dennis, Michael E., and National Geodetic Survey. "Putting the Best 'Foot' Forward: Ending the Era of the U.S. Survey Foot/ Webinar Series/ National Geodetic Survey." noaa.gov, 2019. https://geodesy.noaa.gov/web/science_edu/webinar_series/2019-webinars.shtml

Ferguson, T.J., G. Lennis Berlin, and Leigh J. Kuwanwisiwma. "Kukhepya: Searching for Hopi Trails." In *Landscapes of Movement: Trails, Paths and Roads in Anthropological Perspective*, edited by C.L. Erickson and J.A. Darling, 20–41. Philadelphia: University Museum Publications, 2009.

Figg, Laurann, and Jane Farrell-Beck. "Amputation in the Civil War: Physical and Social Dimensions." *Journal of the History of Medicine and Allied Sciences* 48, no. 4 (1993): 454–75.

Firdaus, Febriana. "The Women of Kendeng Set Their Feet in Cement to Stop a Mine in Their Lands. This Is Their Story." Mongabay Environmental News, November 13, 2020. https://news.mongabay.com/2020/11/the-women-of-kendeng-set-their-feet-in-cement-to-stop-a-mine-in-their-lands-this-is-their-story/.

Fitzgerald, David. "Mr. Rumsfeld's War." In *Learning to Forget: U.S.*

Army Counterinsurgency Doctrine and Practice from Vietnam to Iraq. Stanford: Stanford University Press, 2013.

Gay'wu Group of Women. *Song Spirals: Sharing Women's Wisdom of Country through Songlines.* Crows Nest NSW: Allen & Unwin. Kindle, 2019.

Geissler, Marie. "Contemporary Indigenous Australian Art and Native Title Land Claim." *Arts* 10, no. 32 (May 11, 2021).

Gilbert, Samuel. "Protests Target Spanish Colonial Statues That 'Celebrate Genocide' in US West." *The Guardian*, June 24, 2020.

Ginat, Gitit. "How a Bedouin Tracker Sees the Desert." *Atlas Obscura* (blog), September 2022.

Girvan, Anita. *Carbon Footprints as Cultural-Ecological Metaphors.* Oxford and New York: Routledge. Kindle, 2018.

Godlewska, Anne. "Geography and Cassini IV: Witness and Victim of Social and Disciplinary Change." *Cartographica* 35, no. 3-4 (1998): 25–39.

Goldberger, Paul. *Up from Zero: Politics, Architecture, and the Rebuilding of New York.* New York: Random House, 2004.

Gooch, Pernille. "Feet Following Hooves." In Ingold, Tim, and Jo Lee Vergunst. *Ways of Walking: Ethnography and Practice on Foot.* London and New York: Routledge. Kindle, 2016.

Gordon, Michael R. "The Test for Rumsfeld: Will Strategy Work?" *New York Times*, April 1, 2003, sec. World.

Hay, Richard L., and Mary D. Leakey. "The Fossil Footprints of Laetoli." *Scientific American* 246, no. 2 (February 1982): 50–57.

Heim, R.J. "Co-Creator of Tribute of Light at Ground Zero Reflects on How Iconic Memorial Came About." WJAR, 2022. https://turnto10.com/news/local/co-creator-of-tribute-of-light-at-ground-zero-reflects-on-how-iconic-memorial-came-about.

Heller, Jordan. "An Oral History of the George W. Bush Shoe Throwing, 15 Years Later." *New York Magazine.* Sec. Intelligencer, December 14, 2023.

Herren Rajagopalan, Angela. *Portraying the Aztec Past: The Codices Boturini, Azcatitlan, and Aubin.* First edition. Recovering Lan-

guages and Literacies of the Americas. Austin: University of Texas Press, 2019.
Hidalgo, Alex. *Trail of Footprints*. Austin: University of Texas Press, 2019.
Hopi Tribe et al vs. Donald J. Trump et al 1:17-cv-02590 (December 4, 2017).
Hummels, Mark. "Made Whole Again: New Foot Attached to Oñate Statue." *Albuquerque Journal*, January 17, 1998.
Ingold, Tim. "Footprints through the Weather-World: Walking, Breathing, Knowing." *Journal of the Royal Anthropological Institute* 16, no. S1 (May 2010): S121–39.
Ingold, Tim, and Jo Lee Vergunst. *Ways of Walking: Ethnography and Practice on Foot*. London and New York: Routledge. Kindle, 2016.
International Fund for Animal Welfare (IFAW). "The Impact of Climate Change on Elephants," www.ifaw.org, March 5, 2024.
Jain-Neubauer, Jutta. *Feet and Footwear in Indian Culture*. Toronto: Bata Shoe Museum in association with Mapin Pub. Ahmedabad; New York, 2000.
Jet Propulsion Laboratory. "The Apollo Experiment that Keeps on Giving." NASA Jet Propulsion Laboratory (JPL), www.jpl.nasa.gov. July 24, 2019.
Kennedy, John. "John F. Kennedy Moon Speech—Rice Stadium, September 12, 1962." www.nasa.gov, 2019.
Ko, Dorothy. *Cinderella's Sisters: A Revisionist History of Footbinding*. Berkeley: University of California Press, 2005.
———. *Every Step a Lotus: Shoes for Bound Feet*. Berkeley: University of California Press, 2001.
Kula, Witold. *Measures and Men*. 1986. Reprint, Princeton: Princeton University Press, 2014.
Kuwanwisiwma, Leigh J., and T.J. Ferguson. "Ang Kuktota: Hopi Ancestral Sites and Cultural Landscapes." *Expedition Magazine* 46, no. 2 (2004): 24–29.
Kuwanwisiwma, Leigh J., T.J. Ferguson, and Chip Colwell-Chan-

thaponh, eds. *Footprints of Hopi History*. Tucson: University of Arizona Press, 2018.

Land, Kyle. "Fate of Alcalde Oñate Statue in Limbo." *Albuquerque Journal*, April 18, 2021.

Leakey, Mary D. "Tracks and Tools." *Philosophical Transactions of the Royal Society of London. Series B. Biological Sciences* 292, no. 1057 (May 8, 1981): 95–102.

Libeskind, Daniel, and Sarah Crichton. *Breaking Ground: An Immigrant's Journey from Poland to Ground Zero*. New York: Riverhead Books, 2004.

Lie, Swedian, and Stephanie Tangkilisan. "Episode 26: Kartini Kendeng: Indonesia's Own Water Protectors—Dialogika." Dialogika.id, August 17, 2024. https://dialogika.id/kartini-kendeng/.

Linklater, Andro. *Measuring America: How the United States Was Shaped by the Greatest Land Sale in History*. New York: Walker Publishing Company, 2002.

Llewellyn, Aisyah. "Nusantara: Celebrations Planned in Indonesia's Costly 'Symbol of Progress.'" Al Jazeera. August 16, 2024.

Lower Manhattan Development Corporation (LMDC), "World Trade Center Site Memorial Competition Guidelines," 2003. Archived December 8, 2017 at the Wayback Machine.

Lujan, Fernando M. "Light Footprints: The Future of American Military Intervention." Washington, D.C.: Center for a New American Security, 2013.

Macgregor, Colin. "Preserving the Ancient Human Trackways Site in the Willandra Lakes World Heritage Area." *Studies in Conservation* 67, no. 51 (March 17, 2022): 5150–55.

McGrath, Ann. "People of the Footprints." *Interventions* 24, no. 2 (October 12, 2021): 181–207.

Miller, Paul. "Yugoslav Eulogies: The Footprints of Gavrilo Princip." *The Carl Beck Papers in Russian and East European Studies* 2304, no. 2304 (June 20, 2014).

Milne, A. A., and Ernest H. Shepard. *Winnie-The-Pooh*. 1926. Reprint, New York: Puffin Books/Penguin Books, 1992.

Mitchell, Alanna. "America Has Two Feet. It's about to Lose One of Them." *New York Times*, August 18, 2020, sec. Science.

Montgomerie, T.G. "Report of the Trans-Himalayan Explorations during 1867." *Proceedings of the Royal Geographical Society of London* 13, no. 3 (1868): 183–98.

Montgomerie, T.G., and Pundit. "Report of a Route-Survey Made by Pundit from Nepal to Lhasa, and Thence from the Upper Valley of the Brahmaputra to Its Source." *The Journal of the Royal Geographical Society of London* 38 (1868): 129–219.

Morphy, Frances. "Performing Law: The Yolngu of Blue Mud Bay Meet the Native Title Process." In *The Social Effects of Native Title*, 31–57. Canberra: ANU Press, 2007.

Mundy, Barbara E. *The Mapping of New Spain: Indigenous Cartography and the Maps of the Relaciones Geográficas*. Chicago: University of Chicago Press, 2000.

NASA. "Flag Day – Flying High: The Stars and Stripes in Space," www.nasa.gov, 2013.

National Institute of Standards and Technology (NIST). "U.S. Survey Foot." www.nist.gov, July 26, 2019.

National Oceanic and Atmospheric Administration, noaa.gov. "A Tale of Two Feet." www.noaa.gov, 2017.

Navarrete, Federico. "The Path from Aztlan to Mexico: On Visual Narration in Mesoamerican Codices." *RES: Anthropology and Aesthetics* 37 (2000): 37–48.

New York Times. "Footprints on the Moon: Pictures Brought Back by Apollo 11 Crew." July 30, 1969.

New York Times. "Questions and Answers at the News Conference Held by Apollo 11 Astronauts." August 13, 1969.

New York Times Magazine. "Filling the Void. A Memorial by Paul Myoda and Julian Laverdiere." September 23, 2001.

Nomad Art Productions "Djalkiri: We Are Standing on Their Names, Blue Mud Bay." (2010.) https://www.nomadart.com.au/?p=4045.

Nobel, Philip. *Sixteen Acres: Architecture and the Outrageous Struggle for the Future of Ground Zero*. New York: Metropolitan Books, Henry Holt and Co, 2005.

Oxford English Dictionary (OED), n.d. (Accessed June 9, 2022).

Pangtey, Surendra Singh. *Saga of a Native Explorer: Pundit Nain Singh C.I.E.: Exploration in Forbidden Trans-Himalayan Land of Tibet and Central Asia during 1865–74*. A transliteration of the diaries of Nain

Singh Rawat C.I.E. Dehra Dun: Johar Shauka Varishta, Johar Sanskritik Sanghatan, Bishen Singh, Mahendra Pal Singh, 2017.

Pasek, Anne. "Fixing Carbon: Mediating Matter in a Warming World." PhD. Diss. (New York University, 2019)

Perrot, Capucine. "Mona Hatoum, Performance Still 1985–95." www.tate.org.uk, n.d.

Propp, Wren. "A Giant of Ambivalence." *Albuquerque Journal*, January 25, 2004.

Raj, Kapil. "When Human Travellers Become Instruments: The Indo-British Exploration of Central Asia in the Nineteenth Century." In *Instruments, Travel and Science: Itineraries of Precision from the Seventeenth to the Twentieth Century*, 156–88. London and New York: Routledge, 2003.

Ramadani, Sami. "The Shoes We Longed For." *The Guardian*, December 17, 2008.

Rao, Radhakrishna. "A Firm Footing for the Disabled." *Appropriate Technology*, 2001.

Rensberger, Boyce. "Prehistoric Footprints of Man-like Creatures Found." *New York Times*, March 22, 1979.

Romero, Simon. "Statue's Stolen Foot Reflects Divisions over Symbols of Conquest." *New York Times*, September 30, 2017.

———. "It Takes a Foot Thief." *New York Times*, October 17, 2017.

Ryder, Arthur W. *The Panchatantra*. 1925. Reprint. Chicago: University of Chicago Press, 1956.

Safire, William. "Footprint." *New York Times Magazine*, February 17, 2008.

Schulz, Dana. "The History of Little Syria and an Immigrant Community's Lasting Legacy | 6sqft." 6sqft | NYC Real Estate news and information, 2017, www.6sqft.com.

Seefeldt, Douglas. "Oñate's Foot: Histories, Landscapes, and Contested Memories in the Southwest." *Faculty Publications, Department of History* 25 University of Nebraska-Lincoln (March 22, 2005).

Senie, Harriet. "Commemorating 9/11: From the Tribute in Light to Reflecting Absence." In *Memorials to Shattered Myths: Vietnam to*

9/11, 122–68. Oxford Scholarship Online: Oxford University Press, 2016.

Sengoopta, Chandak, *Imprint of the Raj: How Fingerprinting Was Born in Colonial India*. London: Pan Macmillan, 2003.

Shackle, Samira. "Chainsaws, Disguises and Toxic Tea: The Battle for Sheffield's Trees." *The Guardian*, October 24, 2023.

Slijepcevic, Maja. "Monument and Counter-Monument Sights in Post-Conflict Bosnia and Herzegovina: A Case Study of Gavrilo Princip's Monuments." *Sociology Mind* 6 (2016): 114–29.

Smyth, Edmund. "The Pundit Nain Singh." *The Proceedings of the Royal Geographical Society and Monthly Record of Geography* 4, no. 5 (1882): 315–17.

Solman, Gregory. "BP: Coloring Public Opinion?" Adweek, January 14, 2008.

Srinivasan, Raman. "Technology Sits Cross-Legged." In *Artificial Parts, Practical Lives: Modern Histories of Prosthetics*, 204–13. New York: New York University Press, 2002.

Steigerwald, William. "Laser Beams Reflected between Earth and Moon Boost Science—NASA." www.nasa.gov, August 10, 2020.

Sturcke, James. "Soleful Tribute: Bush Shoe-Throwing Now a Work of Art." *The Guardian*, January 29, 2009.

Sturken, Marita. "Containing Absence, Shaping Presence at Ground Zero." *Memory Studies* 13, no. 3 (June 2020): 313–21.

———. "The 9/11 Memorial Museum and the Remaking of Ground Zero." *American Quarterly* 67, no. 2 (2015): 471–90.

———. "Tourism and 'Sacred Ground': The Space of Ground Zero." In *Tourists of History: Memory, Kitsch and Consumerism from Oklahoma City to Ground Zero*, 165–218. Durham, NC: Duke University Press, 2007. Kindle.

Subramaniam, Kamala. *Srimad Bhagavatam*. 14th edition, 1979. Reprint, Mumbai: Bharatiya Vidya Bhavan, 2016. Kindle.

Supran, Geoffrey, and Naomi Oreskes. "Rhetoric and Frame Analysis of ExxonMobil's Climate Change Communications." *One Earth* 4, no. 5 (May 2021): 696–719.

Szymczyk, Adam, ed. *Ahlam Shibli Trackers*. Cologne: Verlag der Buchhandlung Walther Koenig, 2007.

Tamisari, Franca. "Body, Vision and Movement: In the Footprints of the Ancestors." *Oceania* 68, no. 4 (June 1998): 249–70.

———. "Yolngu Country as a Multidimensional Tangle of Relationships. How 'Everything Is Linked to One Another.'" *Lagoonscapes* 2, no. 1 (July 7, 2022): 93–118.

Topsfield, Jewel. "Women of Rembang Put Their Feet down to Save Farms from Cement Factory." *The Sydney Morning Herald*, May 2016.

Traub, James. "The Empty Threat of 'Boots on the Ground.'" *New York Times Magazine*, January 5, 2016.

Trotter, H. "Account of the Pundit's Journey in Great Tibet from Leh in Ladakh to Lhasa, and of His Return to India via Assam." *Journal of the Royal Geographical Society of London* 47 (January 1, 1877): 86–136.

Trujillo, Michael L. "Oñate's Foot: Remembering and Dismembering in Northern New Mexico." *Aztlán: A Journal of Chicano Studies* 33, no. 2 (2008): 91–119.

Turnbull, David. "Cartography and Science in Early Modern Europe: Mapping the Construction of Knowledge Spaces." *Imago Mundi* 48, no. 1 (January 1996): 5–24.

U.S. Immigration and Customs Enforcement. "ICE Shadow Wolves." www.ice.gov, n.d.

Van Doren, Benjamin M., Kyle G. Horton, Adriaan M. Dokter, Holger Klinck, Susan B. Elbin, and Andrew Farnsworth. "High-Intensity Urban Light Installation Dramatically Alters Nocturnal Bird Migration." *Proceedings of the National Academy of Sciences* 114, no. 42 (October 2, 2017): 1175–80.

Vanderpool, Tim. "Native Trackers: 'Secret Weapon' in Drug War." *Christian Science Monitor*, July 18, 2002.

Wackernagel, Mathis, and William Rees. *Our Ecological Footprint:*

Reducing Human Impact on Earth. Philadelphia: New Society Publishers, 1996.
Waller, Derek. *The Pundits*. Lexington: University Press of Kentucky. Kindle, 1990.
Wanambi, Wukun, Henry Skerritt, and Kade McDonald. *Madayin: Eight Decades of Aboriginal Art Painting from Yirrkala*. Kluge-Ruhe Aboriginal Art Collection of the University of Virginia and DelMonico Books, 2022.
Watchdoc Documentary. "SAMIN vs SEMEN (English Subtitled)." YouTube, April 4, 2017. https://www.youtube.com/watch?v=CY-bXvOGYRuU.
Watts, Linda S. "Reflecting Absence or Presence? Public Space and Historical Memory at Ground Zero." *Space and Culture* 12, no. 4 (November 2009): 412–18.
Webb, Steve, Matthew L. Cupper, and Richard Robins. "Pleistocene Human Footprints from the Willandra Lakes, Southeastern Australia." *Journal of Human Evolution* 50, no. 4 (April 2006): 405–13.
WGBH. "NOVA, to the Moon; Interview with Buzz Aldrin, Engineer and Astronaut, and Lunar Module Pilot on Apollo 11, Part 4 of 4." Boston, MA: GBH Archives, 1998.
———. "NOVA, to the Moon; Interview with Dr. David 'Dave' J. Roddy, Astrogeologist at the US Geological Survey, Part 2 of 2." Boston MA: GBH Archives, 1998.
Wheeler, Mark. "Shadow Wolves." *Smithsonian Magazine* 33, no. 10 (January 2003): 40–47.
White Cube. "Mona Hatoum at the Millennium Gallery, Sheffield." www.whitecube.com, April 18, 2018.
Wilford, John Noble. "Prints Show a Modern Foot in Prehumans." *New York Times*, February 26, 2009.
Wyatt, Edward. "Pataki's Surprising Limit on Ground Zero Design." *New York Times*, July 2, 2002, sec. New York.

ABOUT np:

Dedicated to the formation of the social and economic combinations of new presses, the nonprofit np: (np-press.org) creates new institutionally-based publishing units. It questions how innovation comes about in scholarly publishing, given the speed of technological change and the quickly modified forms by which knowledge is arrived at and sustained. Many publishers continue to over-rely on outmoded communication technologies and assumptions about what content is and how it is generated. np: is designed specifically to circumvent the problematic nature of publication as we know it, including not simply the way current practices shape scholarship but also the tendency toward reproducing inequality and exclusion. As part of its program, np: publishes, hosts, and supports work that interrogates the university system and its sedimented histories, from land acquisition to student debt. np:'s standpoint is decisively outside the university press framework and so activates new perspectives on academic labor, knowledge production, and modes of resistance.

www.ingramcontent.com/pod-product-compliance
Lightning Source LLC
Chambersburg PA
CBHW021936160426
43195CB00011B/1109